CVAC

NOV - - 2020

Local Dirt

Local Dirt

SEASONAL RECIPES FOR **EATING CLOSE TO HOME**

Andrea Bemis

Harper WAVE

An Imprint of HarperCollinsPublishers

HarperCollins books may be purchased for educational, business, or
sales promotional use. For information, please email the Special Markets
Department at SPsales@harpercollins.com.

FIRST EDITION

Designed by Leah Carlson-Stanisic

Food photography by Andrea Bemis

Farm photography by Kate Schwager

Lifestyle photography by Modoc Stories

Library of Congress Cataloging-in-Publication Data

Names: Bemis, Andrea, author.
Title: Local dirt / Andrea Bemis.
Description: First edition. | New York, NY: Harper Wave, 2020. |
Includes index.
Identifiers: LCCN 2020012441 (print) | LCCN
2020012442 (ebook) | ISBN 9780062970275 (hardback) |
ISBN 9780062970282 (ebook)
Subjects: LCSH: Cooking, American. | Seasonal cooking. | Cook-
books.
Classification: LCC TX715 .B4657 2020 (print) | LCC TX715
(ebook) | DDC 641.5973—dc23
LC record available at https://lccn.loc.gov/2020012441
LC ebook record available at https://lccn.loc.gov/2020012442

20 21 22 23 24   TC   10 9 8 7 6 5 4 3 2 1

Our hands can plant the seeds
of peace, community, love, and hope.
Pepper, my sweet girl, welcome
to the dirty life.

Contents

Author's Note

This journey began one morning in the spring of 2018, when I opened my pantry to grab a can of coconut milk and had an epiphany. I stared at that little tin and thought, *I have no idea where this came from. Who the heck picked these coconuts? Who packaged them? And how did this can end up in my pantry?* I looked at the other products on my shelves—rice vinegar, tahini, olive oil, my beloved avocados, everything in my spice drawer—and had the same thought, over and over again. I had a vague idea of some of their origins, but that was about it, and suddenly I was hungry for knowledge.

It occurred to me that the three qualities I value most when it comes to food go something like this: wellness (is it good for my body?), sustainability (is it good for the planet?), and community (is it good for other people?). These qualities become a lot harder to evaluate when a food's origin is unknown or distant. I began to wonder if there was a way to bring the elements of that triple bottom line together through eating local food. My curiosity became overwhelming, and I started asking myself more questions I didn't have answers to: Can I find the same beneficial fats I get from avocados and almonds from foods grown closer to home? What are those foods? Where are they, and how and when are they grown? What farmers or foragers or ranchers are providing them? And can I find answers to these questions through eating locally?

For a decade now, my husband, Taylor, and I have made our living as vegetable farmers. I've written about our lives and my farm-to-table creations on my blog, *Dishing Up the Dirt*, and in my first cookbook of the same name. During my years as a farmer and a cook, I've begun to realize that I'm actually searching for something deeper through food, something more than sustenance or enjoyment alone. I think that instinct is what led me to farming in the first place, and it's driven me to make various choices about food ever since. It's why I steered away from dairy and meat for a long time—I was concerned about their effects on my health as well as the effects of their production on our planet. It's why I began playing around in the kitchen with making alternatives to dairy products using cashews and miso instead. And it's why I've now come full circle and started raising pigs and chickens on our farm and buying cheese, yogurt, milk, beef, rabbit, and lamb from other farmers and ranchers and producers in our community. I'm no longer convinced that meat and dairy are harmful to my health, and I want to support the folks who are producing these foods responsibly. But through all of these changes to my perspective on food, I still haven't been able to put my finger on what exactly I'm looking for.

Coming from a small farming community, I had long considered myself a locavore. But there was a lot I didn't know about where Taylor and I live in north central Oregon, and what bounties there are to be had here. I love tasting the flavors of the world, but at a time when our food system seems to be failing us, a time when big food and big agriculture and corporate grocery store culture have erased the world's seasons and most people can't trace their food back to the humans that grew it—this feeling deep in my gut told me that I needed to go back to basics. I began to realize that maybe what I've been looking for all these years is a more personal connection to my landscape, to my community, and ultimately to myself. In my journey to deepen my relationship to food, I've been trying to find my way home.

I knew I wasn't alone in this regard. Food is at the center of our lives, whether we're farmers or lawyers or doctors or teachers. Most people I know are trying to eat well for themselves, their communities, and the planet, but it's not always easy to know what to do. When I started learning about other folks' journeys with eating locally, I decided to give myself a challenge: For thirty days of September, I would source all my ingredients from within a two-hundred-mile radius of our farm. Thirty days. Two hundred miles. Local food from local dirt. I hoped that in doing so, I would find a more grounded sense of place and a community of folks that I never knew existed.

I did find those things. And in the end, I found so much more.

Those thirty days changed everything: how I feel; how I eat; my relationships with my family, my community, and my landscape. How I think about my place in the world. As I charted this journey (which we coined "the local thirty") via my blog and Instagram, folks from all across North America joined in, and it changed them too. I stepped out of my comfort zone and encouraged others to do the same—to be bold and curious and start asking questions. Ask your chicken farmer at the local green market if you can go visit their operation. Ask an employee at your grocery store if they have time to explain the supply chain of the produce they sell. Invite yourself over to dinner at the house of a neighbor who eats differently than you do. Take no for an answer if that's what it is, but they might just surprise you and say yes.

For me, this was a journey about strangers becoming friends. I butchered my first pig under the guidance of a local pig farmer, who taught me how to make bacon. I experienced the biggest thrill of my life crossing the Columbia River Bar in an albacore tuna dayboat and then spent an entire day out on the open ocean with three fishermen who were strangers to me then and who now will be forever dear to me. Taylor and I finally visited the ranch of the fourth-generation beef rancher that neighbors our vegetable booth at the farmers' market, watched teenagers ride the mechanical bull at the County Fair, and grilled up some burgers to enjoy with Coors Light for dinner. It wasn't about the beef. It wasn't about the cheap beer that I don't normally drink or the ingredients we served with it. It was about this man that we were getting to know and love, about connecting with parts of our community we'd never visited. It was about so much more than two hundred miles. My journey was actually about going to see what home means to the people who produce all the foods that make up my corner of the world.

Eating locally, for me, is about discovering and celebrating what we have, not mourning what we're missing. This cookbook re-creates a place that existed not that long ago, where we only had access to ingredients that came from our home, or our neighbors' homes, and we knew and loved the people who provided them. The spirit of this book is exactly what J. B. Mackinnon and Alisa Smith captured in a single word in the title of their

The local thirty journey was pushing me out of my comfort zone and into memorable experiences with new people, new landscapes, and damn good food.

local eating guide, *Plenty*. When we start looking around and talking to each other, we quickly realize that we have so much. Eating the foods I found and prepared rooted me deeper into my home. These ingredients had a story to tell: They were the result of hardworking hands and determined hearts. They were the flesh of plants I touched and animals I knew. I found out that eating locally is about discovering and celebrating a bounty that is all our own and letting it shape a little bit of who we are. It made me feel wilder, more alive, more connected. More joyful and more grateful.

This cookbook commemorates that experience through my stories about learning how to fully live within a two-hundred-mile radius of my home; stories of the growers and the makers I discovered who produce the foods that sustain my little family; and the recipes I've dreamed up to inspire a simple and beautiful local diet throughout the year. Ultimately it's a book about slowing down, learning, discovering. And whether or not you choose to eat within a two-hundred-mile radius of your home, the recipes in these pages are accessible and adaptable to any cook, in any part in the country.

Most of all, I hope that, no matter where you live, you'll be inspired to cook your own way home.

How to Use This Book

The recipes in this book make use of ingredients that I was able to find locally in the Pacific Northwest. Feel free to follow the recipes as they are written or adapt them to use only ingredients that are local to you. You'll notice that in a lot of recipe ingredient lists I reference "cooking fat." What is intended here is to use whatever fat you've got on hand—such as butter, lard, bacon fat, oil, or ghee. They can all be used interchangeably in most cases when it comes to sautéing veggies or preparing meat. In each recipe you'll find a guide on how to make substitutions, including what you can expect to find at your local farmers' market or grocery store. These recipes are meant to be a blueprint for you to customize—swapping in, swapping out, adding a little bit of this, or taking away what you don't have. They're very forgiving and were created with the idea that you can make them your own with what you've got.

Every cook, every kitchen, and every ingredient is going to be a little different. So know that when you're cooking in your own oven, the food you make may look and taste a little different from the descriptions in a cookbook. And that's fine! My general approach to cooking is to not take it super seriously, because cooking and eating should be fun. Taste-test as you go and enjoy yourself.

At the end of this book I've included resources to help you learn how to locate your nearest farmers' market, apply for food stamps that you can use at farmers' markets if you qualify, purchase whole animals at a good cost, and find local grains or dairy. Check out page 289 for how to do this in the region you call home.

Introduction

The month of September started off in the most terrifying way (for me, that is): sixty miles offshore in the Pacific Ocean with three fishermen of the Tre-Fin Day Boat Tuna Company, whom I'd met only minutes before hopping aboard their small commercial fishing boat. As a woman who doesn't swim well and is generally nervous around large bodies of water, this wasn't a situation I ever imagined I'd be in. But I was determined to experience firsthand how one of my favorite fish ends up on my table. After all, this was what my experiment with eating locally was supposed to be about: stepping out of my comfort zone and fully embracing new experiences, new places, and new people.

As I climbed on board their boat, one of the fishermen asked if I tend to get seasick. *Seasick?* I thought. I couldn't recall a time in my life when I was in a situation where seasickness was an option. Good, they said, because we don't turn the boat around for anything. We're out here until we catch our fish, run out of bait, or it gets dark on us. This conversation took place at six in the morning. It wouldn't be dark for twelve more hours. I was hoping they'd catch those fish first, before the other things happened. My stomach knotted up a bit, and panic set in. We hadn't even left the dock, and I was already second-guessing this whole local experiment. Maybe I could have just interviewed these guys on land instead of actually going to work with them? But within minutes, we were on our way and I was in it for the long haul.

Getting out into the open sea meant crossing the Columbia River Bar, one of the most dangerous water passages in the world. I kept a close eye on the expressions of the fishermen around me. Everyone was quiet, the captain focused and serious. I white-knuckled the giant beanbag I was sitting on, which helps absorb the shocks of the waves. The passage was bumpy as hell, and after each climb up a gigantic swell, our tiny boat would crash down into rough water nose-first. Again and again, we'd climb, crash, climb, crash. I was waiting for the boat to split in half. After what felt like hours, we found ourselves in calmer water. It was the first time I'd been on a boat in the ocean and couldn't see land. I felt alone and vulnerable but tried not to let it show on my face.

But my fears started to fade away once the nerves from crossing the bar began to wear off. Eventually, sixty miles out, we slowed down and it was still kind of wavy but not treacherous. After talking to the guys for a while, waiting for the fish to show up, I started to actually enjoy myself. Here we were, four people on a boat, so close in the middle of nowhere, the stakes so high that trust was mandatory. As we talked, we discovered that we had a lot in common. Each day, we were all out there providing food for our communities, though I joked with them about the obvious truth—picking kale is way less harrowing.

Tre-Fin started with an idea—that a Pacific Northwest albacore fishery maybe doesn't have to totally rely on the international market. I had no idea that almost all the albacore tuna I purchase at the grocery store is probably caught right there in my local waters but then shipped to China or Indonesia for processing and packaging before being sent back to our neighborhood grocery shelves. That supply chain just doesn't make sense and doesn't sit well with the fishermen that I was on board with. So these guys do things a little differently. Instead of going out for days or weeks at a time—which is how most large-scale commercial boats operate—they go out for just a day at a time and pack their catch in ice to cool it down for the trip home in the evening. This approach makes for a lot of bumpy early-morning bar crossings. Once their catch arrives back on the dock, they process it by hand into its best cuts and package it. Loins and loin medallions go into the freezer in vacuum-sealed bags while the less choice cuts are put into pouches as "canned" tuna. They sell the fish at farmers' markets in the greater Portland area and also run a small CSF (Community Supported Fishery). They're committed to doing things the local way, because they feel it's better for the product, the environment, and the consumer—but it's also the hard way.

In terms of how to catch an albacore, I learned the process, all right. When I hopped on board the boat, I didn't expect that I would actually be reeling in fish. But when the guys needed the extra hand, I had to jump right into action. I was nervous that I'd lose the fish or, worse yet, let go of the rod, but not helping felt as unnatural as sitting on the couch watching TV while Taylor harvests carrots. Before I knew it, albacore were flying into the boat. It was go-time—so intense, with a loud and crazy sense of urgency. But as we started reeling in fish, netting them, stunning them, and making kills, I felt a sort of rhythm cutting through all that chaos. It made me feel at home, because it happens on the farm, too. This dreamy awareness of what Taylor's doing, whether he's right next to me stuffing starts into the ground or a quarter mile away up at the top of the field on the tractor. Knowing where he'll be next. And him knowing where I'll be. That's how these guys were as they started catching fish, and I had to do it, too—everyone jumping around each other, under this line, over that one, tossing nets around, pulling fish. Everyone knows each other's move before they do. Your awarenesses blend and your rhythms are connected because they have to be for the whole thing to work. You have to function as a single unit, or everything falls apart. So, out there in the Pacific Ocean, I felt this unexpected common thread between fishing and farming. You have to do the dance. Go together, be one, or it just won't work.

But what hit me most was a sense of respect for these men, who risk their lives every day and push through long hours of hard work, intense focus, and unpredictable conditions to bring ethical food from our local waters to people's plates. Spending time with them became about much more than just educating myself on sustainable fishing practices or local food. It became about developing a deeper appreciation of their integrity, of the common threads we share, of their willingness to welcome me with open arms, put a rod in my hand, and give me the opportunity to experience one of the most thrilling moments of my life: reeling in a thirty-pound fish.

Once my newfound friends and I returned safely to land, we got to kick back with a few cold beers and a delicious dinner. It really was the best tuna I've ever eaten. Sitting there in the bunkhouse kitchen surrounded by crusty tattooed fishermen eating raw albacore, I was profoundly grateful. The local thirty journey was pushing me out of my comfort zone and into memorable experiences with new people, new landscapes, and damn good food.

About a week after being back home in the dirt, and after finally kick-

ing that swaying-back-and-forth feeling, I found myself in the total opposite direction of the Pacific Ocean. On a hot late-summer afternoon, Taylor and I walked into the Sherman County Fair, on our way out to visit our friends Tim and Keely Jefferies, who own a cattle ranch just down the way from the fairgrounds. Jefferies Ranch Beef had been our neighboring vendors at the farmers' market for over six years, and in our quest to learn more about the beef we'd been eating all that time, we wanted to get a glimpse of what life was like just east of our farm.

Tim grew up in Sherman County and spent a good chunk of his younger years roping on the rodeo circuit, so naturally we wanted to swing by the fair on our way to the ranch and see the cowboys in action. On our drive, I found myself thinking about how we'd never had an occasion to visit the nearby county, which is so close to us in distance yet so far from home both environmentally and culturally. In the early fall, the land is dry and harsh—pretty bleak from our perspective as outsiders from lusher landscapes. Our farm in the Hood River Valley is nestled between irrigated pastures and orchards—everything is green year-round. Sherman County is all dryland wheat farming and cattle range. It's a place I've always thought of as kind of desolate, but as Taylor and I drove into the fairgrounds, I caught myself appreciating its unique beauty.

At the fair, we stuck out like sore thumbs. This was a place where everyone knew everyone. And we're from a town where everyone knows everyone, so we know what it's like when someone's sitting at the local pub who isn't from around there. Taylor and I are farmers, yes, so there was a lot of dirt on our jeans. But it was different dirt and they were different jeans from the ones these cowboys were wearing.

As soon as we got to the fair, we were offered a bag of caramel corn—and while it didn't fit my criteria for eating locally, we accepted it graciously (another one of our rules during this challenge was to not be an asshole). We were treated to a roping lesson from a pro and got to see all the kids proudly show off the 4-H animals they'd raised, which were named primarily after rappers—Ice-T, Salt-N-Pepa, Jay-Z, Snoop Dogg. I knew most of the folks at the fair grew up differently from me—we probably vote very differently—but what I loved the most about that day was that none of those differences really

mattered. We were welcomed with open arms, and we weren't even judged for how terrible we were at roping. Being at the fair made me appreciate Tim that much more.

After we kicked the dust off our boots, we continued out to the ranch to meet up with Tim, Keely, and their son Jack. We brought a little bit of our own farm with us: greens for a salad and some sweet peppers to toss on the grill. Tim made the burgers. Keely made some simple side dishes and zucchini bread for dessert. We drank beer and enjoyed this honest meal with a view: Over the golden wheat fields, we could just make out three Cascade volcanoes—Jefferson, Hood, and Adams—through the smoky haze. Keely talked about the challenges of being a beef rancher in recent years, as health concerns about red meat have grown. Luckily, she said, consumers' newfound awareness of and appreciation for grass-fed and -finished beef has been good for sales, and she's seeing a shift in people's values about food. She feels that "clean eating" is more than just a trend. Today there is an uptick in demand for meat that has been raised sustainably and humanely—which is how the Jefferies family does it.

They told us that when times were tough, they didn't eat their own meat because they couldn't afford it. Instead they swung by drive-throughs for quick burgers and relied for many years on wild game that they hunted—elk and deer mostly. Then one year, an animal in their cattle herd got injured and they couldn't sell it, so they decided to keep the meat for their freezer. Tim smiled and, with this twinkle he can get in his eyes, said, "We've never eaten wild game since."

What I learned from the Jefferies family is that beef is complicated. The industry on a whole is super flawed. But then you get to know actual ranchers like Keely and Tim, and whether you eat beef or not, it's clear that they're stewards of this beautiful country. Ranchers rely on healthy, productive land in order to stay in business with healthy cattle. More than 40 percent of the land in the United States is pasture or rangeland—too rocky, steep, or arid to support cultivated agriculture. Well-managed cattle grazing mimics native large mammal grazing, improves the water-holding capacity of the land, and increases biodiversity. And rangelands preserve vast swaths of habitat across the West. A food system without animals is simply unhealthy and unsustainable. Regenerative farming is essential to a healthy ecosystem, and that includes grazing animals. Sure, there are plenty of bad actors in the cattle business, like any other business, but the Jefferies family and their neighbors know their land and how to manage it to its best capacity. Without them out here, invasive weeds would likely take over.

Over the years of getting to know Tim and Keely Jefferies at the farmers' market, we've had a standing tradition that unless someone has a wedding or a funeral to attend, we go get a beer afterward at the same damn bar we've been going to together since the start. Our conversations are so simple and so real: what's happening at the ranch, how the veggie farming is going, what battles with deer or flea beetles or wildfire or coyotes we're fighting. That tradition stands, and it was so special to bring our worlds even closer with our visit out to Sherman County.

In mid-September, when it really started to feel like fall and we were drinking our coffee in the dark, Taylor, I, and my brother Adam ventured up to Trout Lake, Washington, thirty miles northeast of Tumbleweed, in search of fresh milk. We'd heard of Mountain Laurel Jerseys Dairy from friends, and we were eager to meet farmer Jesse, who happened to be kind enough to let us help him milk the ladies at dawn. I'd never milked a cow before and wasn't quite sure what to expect. I'd seen documentaries about the horrors of dairy farms, and though I knew Mountain Laurel was a small, organic production, I was still half expecting to encounter quite a bit of chaos.

Jesse led us out to the pasture to wrangle the girls into the barn so they could line up for milking. I'd honestly never seen anything like it: Jesse didn't need to do a darn thing. With his calm nature, the cows just seemed to trust him and know the drill. They quietly lined up, and we were able to aid in the morning milking session. I had never tasted milk straight from a cow before, but dang, there was life before fresh milk, and there is now life after fresh milk. It was rich and sweet and tasted almost like it had been steamed, slightly frothy and comfortingly warm. When it hit my lips, I immediately knew I was done for. We joined Mountain Laurel's "herd share" and now get fresh raw milk weekly.

After milking chores were complete, the four of us filled up pint-sized mason jars with fresh milk, sat on a few hay bales, and chatted about all things

By the end of the thirty days, there was one thing I knew for sure: We were never going back.

dairy farming. We learned that Mountain Laurel is a fourth-generation dairy that began as a homestead claim in 1883. Jesse's great-grandfather Charles founded the farm in the early 1900s to provide residents of the Columbia Gorge (an area just east of Portland) with local butter. Since 2015, Jesse and his family have offered the community local raw milk, which is rare in Washington and not authorized for Oregon producers. There's a lot of information out there about the dangers and benefits of raw milk, and I'm no expert on any of it. I just figured the best way for me to gather information was to visit the farm and production facility myself and talk directly to the farmers. These guys take a lot of care to make sure their customers are getting the safest, freshest product possible, and at their small scale, it's easy for them to control every piece of the process. The result is I can rest easy drinking milk that's got all the good stuff still in it that pasteurization removes.

Our weekly visit to farmer Jesse got a little more exciting late one September morning. We arrived to grab our usual jug of milk and left with a deposit on a puppy. It seems impulsive, yes, but every time we'd pulled up to the farm, we'd been greeted by the most gentle, friendly dog. On this particular morning, we told Jesse how much we adored his dog. "Funny enough you say that. Today, she just had a litter of puppies last week. Do you want to go and see them?" I immediately nodded my head yes, Taylor shook his head no, and the rest is history. We still go out for our weekly gallon of milk, only instead of one dog riding in the back of our car, there are now two.

Some of my experiences during the local thirty were really grand—my tuna boat adventure was hard to beat. But one of the most heartwarming and important chapters for me was having our good friend, farmer, and butcher Michael harvest our pigs for us. We raise pigs on our farm, and in years past, we've sent them off to slaughter. While we brought them to a local meat processor who does a great job, loading up the pigs and taking them to a strange environment for the last day of their lives was stressful for all of us. It just never felt like the best we could do for them when they were giving us everything.

We had bought our piglets from Michael in the spring. They spent their time mud-bathing, sun-basking, chasing each other around, and munching on all our farmers' market leftovers. That fall, Michael was getting set up to process his own pork, so it felt right to have him come over to complete the circle for us. Michael does what he does because he loves animals, and his animal husbandry was more honorable than I ever thought possible. Watching how respectful he was with each animal, before, during, and after it died—how he touched it and handled it—filled me with gratitude. Even though we always knew we were going to harvest them, these girls were our buddies, and it was a difficult day. Knowing that they were happy right up to the moment they stopped living meant a lot to us.

In the end, so many members of our community rallied behind us. Our local watering hole, Solera Brewery, didn't want us to go thirsty, so they created a beer made entirely from local ingredients. Jure from the White Salmon bakery gave us all the resources we needed to find local flours so that I could bake my own bread. And for the entire month before I learned to make sourdough, I paid the damn two-dollar toll both ways to cross the Columbia River to go to the bakery to buy his incredible bread. Our neighborhood donut house, Want Donut, created a delicious Local Thirty donut. I even got to go out to Syncline, one of my favorite local wineries, to harvest Syrah grapes from their vineyard and crush them with my bare feet.

As I shared this journey with our online community, I was inspired to see folks from all different parts of the country creating their own local meals and adventures. Undertaking this challenge in real time alongside so many others who were documenting their experiences reinforced the reason I got myself into this in the first place—my hunch that getting a little bit closer to our food helps us get a little bit closer to each other. By the end of the thirty days, there was one thing I knew for sure: We were never going back.

Our month of eating locally started off with a beautiful dinner that eased any self-doubts (or pity) that we had going into this experiment. It was eye opening, really, to look down at our bowls and know exactly what, where, and who had grown the ingredients that we were about to devour. As we quietly ate, savoring each bite, I had an epiphany: I said out loud to the farm crew, "We're eating like our grandparents did." And it was divine. This first meal was a great way to kick off the local thirty experiment. As it turned out, we weren't going to starve and, better yet, I had a feeling we'd be eating like kings.

Zucchini, Sausage & White Bean Soup

SERVES 6

1 pound dried white beans (105 miles)
1 pound ground pork (0 miles)
1–2 tablespoons olive oil (105 miles)
2 yellow onions, finely chopped (0 miles)
4 garlic cloves, finely chopped (0 miles)
5 cups bone broth (12 miles)
2 quarts water, divided (0 miles)
1 (3-by-2-inch) cheese rind (39 miles)
2 teaspoons salt (157 miles)
½ teaspoon black pepper (a cheat of ours and mileage unknown)

1 teaspoon finely chopped fresh rosemary (0 miles)
1 teaspoon finely chopped fresh thyme (0 miles)
2 medium-sized zucchini, sliced into half moons (0 miles)
1 large bunch of kale, torn into bite-sized pieces (0 miles)
Grated cheese for serving (39 miles)
Crusty bread for dunking (18 miles)
Red wine for sipping (20 miles)

Cover beans with water by 2 inches in a pot and bring to a boil. Remove from the heat and let stand, uncovered, for 1 hour. Drain beans in a colander and rinse.

Brown the pork in a large Dutch oven or soup pot until no longer pink. Use a slotted spoon to remove the pork and drain on paper towels.

Add a little olive oil to the pan and cook the onions until softened, about 5 minutes. Add the garlic and cook, stirring, for about 1 minute longer. Add the beans, broth, 1 quart water, cheese rind, salt, pepper, rosemary, and thyme, and simmer, uncovered, until the beans are just tender, about 50 minutes.

Stir in the zucchini and simmer for about 5 minutes. Add the kale, pork, and remaining quart of water and simmer, uncovered, stirring occasionally, for 10–15 minutes longer. Season with more salt and pepper to taste.

Serve with freshly grated cheese, a loaf of hearty bread, and a glass of red wine.

An Ode to American Cuisine

The recipes in this book are a little bit more down-home than I've cooked in the past, and I thought I should explain why.

When I no longer had access to many of the international ingredients I love because they're not available locally (soy sauce, tahini, coconut milk, and so many spices, to name a few) I started to wonder: *What is American cuisine?* I love exploring the flavors of the world and finding new and interesting ways to combine them, but I realized I'd been in an identity crisis for years about my own culture's food.

Throughout my quest to discover new people, new landscapes, and new ingredients, I found myself longing for the food that I grew up eating. My dad's macaroni and cheese is probably the best thing I've ever tasted. I wanted the comfort and nourishment of my grandma's simple dishes like meatloaf, chicken soup, and apple pie.

Here's what's interesting: I gave up all those foods years ago, ostensibly out of concern for my health. I remember being afraid to eat certain things because I read they might be bad for me or the environment. I swore off gluten for a while, and I was basically vegan for two years because I was convinced that all dairy was harmful. With one click of a button, any "superfood" could be delivered to my doorstep in a matter of days. I would add a dozen exotic ingredients to my morning smoothies, convinced I was doing the right thing for my body. I continued to support the industrialized food system because I needed my avocados, coconut milk, and acai concentrate . . . in Oregon.

While I have no regrets, I have to admit I lost my way a little bit. I only felt more isolated with these blanket eating plans, because they had no connection to who I am and where I live. Wellness is a different type of monoculture, and I think it is the opposite of resilience. Through my local food journey, I've experienced how a simple American diet based on local, whole foods might be a better solution than these one-size-fits-all wellness prescriptions. I've seen how, when we eat locally, we connect with ourselves and each other. We feel better and have more energy. We learn to make the most of what we have and constantly adapt to changes in the availability of ingredients throughout the year. Supporting your local producers who you know are trying to make an honest living on their farms and ranches stewarding their animals and crops feels really good. When you're basing your diet off global superfoods, you lose traceability to the knowledge of whether those things are grown in a way that you support.

I believed that the foods I grew up eating were unhealthy and full of processed ingredients—and that's true if you buy them in a box. But before they were mass-produced and made available in the freezer aisle, they were born from American farmers, homesteaders, and homemakers using the ingredients that were grown, raised, hunted, or gathered through hard work and dirty hands. In those days, the rich and hearty foods that became American classics were chock-full of the nutrients and fiber people needed to get them through the day.

In discovering my local ingredients, I started cooking up all the dishes that my grandma made for me. Some of my favorite moments since starting my local food journey have been grilling corn in the heat of the summer, eating a flaky pot pie on the first cool August night, having a slice of buttered pumpkin bread in the fall on a Sunday morning, and warming up on my back porch in the midday winter sun with a big steaming bowl of pot roast in my lap. In a way, by limiting myself to sourcing food only from my home, I went back in time. I went back to an era before food became industrialized, and that's where many classic American dishes come from. It feels good to have found my way to these meals, and I'm so proud to have re-created these recipes on my home turf.

American cuisine used to be about making nourishing food with what you had, though we all know we've strayed pretty far from that simple ethos. It's hard to pinpoint the beginning of food industrialization, but when the commercial canning process was invented in the 1800s, it outsourced food preservation beyond the household. Instead of canning goods with your neighbors to prepare for winter, you could spend that time working for wages and buy canned food at the grocery store. After we got through the food shortages of the Great Depression and World War II, processed food was widely embraced all across the country. You no longer had to know or care where your food came from. Farms got bigger and bigger and were owned by fewer and fewer people. Insect poisons and synthetic fertilizers were used to squeeze more out of the land. Livestock were moved from farms to factories, where their waste kept building, and the ones that survived were the ones that responded best to antibiotics. Canned, frozen, and fast food made it possible to eat cheaply and easily while people spent their time doing other things.

The companies behind processed and fast food latched onto the classic American dishes that they knew would sell. That's how beef stew made it into a can on a shelf and how chicken pot pie ended up in a box. When you think about it this way, it's easy to challenge the notion that American food lacks nutrition and meaning. The standard American diet doesn't have to be highly processed, because it didn't start that way. In fact, American cuisine can be incredibly nourishing and satisfying, and doesn't have to travel far at all.

There are people who are doing it right in my community. They're producing meat, vegetables, fish, fruit, dairy, beans, oil, honey, nuts, vinegar, and grains. They're producing a whole diet. For me, eating clean has become really simple: Supporting my local producers has kept me feeling well and healthy. And these old recipes from the past have bubbled up in my kitchen through the local ingredients available to me. What was beautiful about sharing my journey on social media was finding that other people living in and around rural communities had similar results. And while it wasn't as easy for folks in places like west Texas, eastern Montana, and Arizona as it was for me in the Pacific Northwest, people were able to find local producers that they didn't know existed. These are places that I had thought of as food deserts, but I watched people make a go of it and surprise themselves. "Local" can mean statewide, it can be regional, it can be defined however you need to define it.

The recipes in this book include local, nourishing versions of national standards along with some new, fresh, and simple ways to prepare meat,

The standard American diet doesn't have to be highly processed, because it didn't start that way.

dairy, vegetables, and grains. You'll find old classics that you or your parents might have grown up with, plus some new twists inspired by my local food experience. Chicken pot pie, steak and potato kebabs, biscuits and gravy, fried green tomatoes, huckleberry pancakes, meatloaf, pot roast, grilled cheese and tomato soup, asparagus bundles wrapped in bacon, and strawberry shortcake are just a few of my favorites. You'll also find recipes that don't fit in any classic category, but emerged as tasty combinations of the local ingredients I had on hand. There's a marinated beet, bread, and herb salad; butternut squash chowder, tuna steaks with green sauce, grilled peaches with ricotta and thyme, creamy celeriac soup with pancetta and toasted hazelnuts, grilled steak with a radish and pea shoot slaw, braised leeks with walnuts and bacon, and a frittata for every season.

The spirit of this book is connectedness. I hope it encourages you to get out there, get to know what grows in your region, and get to know your people. Take what you will and what you can and, most of all, celebrate your home.

Advice for Eating Local

Here are some of the tips and tricks that set me up for success on my thirty-day challenge, as well as a longer-term lifestyle shift:

1 **Go in on stuff with friends.** If a CSA share is too much for you, share it with another family member or friends. Divide and conquer. If you can't make it to the market, cover a friend's gas money and give them a list to do it for you. Get them back the next week. Go in on a meat share or a whole animal. Work with each other.

2 **Ask all the questions.** One of the biggest challenges I faced was sourcing cooking staples like oil, salt and pepper, spices, citrus, and grains. But with the help of the internet, social media, and asking ALL THE QUESTIONS, I was able to find what I needed, for the most part. And when I couldn't? I allowed myself a few exceptions (see "Worth the Journey," page 32).

3 **Chest freezers are rad.** For so many reasons. They allow you to buy and store a quarter, half, or full animal from a local farmer at a lower price than if you bought all of that in individual cuts. We stockpiled our own pork as well as local beef, albacore tuna, and chicken in our chest freezer. Every morning while I'm drinking my first cup of coffee, I go out to the freezer and pick one item to put in the fridge to thaw. Each package takes a couple of days, but when you put something new in the fridge every day, there is a constant rotation of thawed meat ready to go for your dinner. Chicken thighs tonight, tuna loin tomorrow, burgers on Friday. Also, freezing fresh food is the easiest way to preserve it. In addition to pretty much any kind of meat, most fruits and veggies keep very well in the freezer, and it's merely a matter of packaging them in freezer bags or paper and tossing them in there. (A lot easier than sanitizing jars and firing up your pressure canner for an afternoon, but I'm all for that too if you have the time.) You can get a small chest freezer at your local appliance store for less than two hundred dollars. If you're living in a small space, double up and use the chest freezer as a countertop too. Big ones are more expensive, but the value they add by allowing you to preserve a large amount of food is well worth it.

4 Cooking locally is about getting back to basics. I sometimes overcomplicate recipes or add too many ingredients. Don't get me wrong, getting creative in the kitchen is one of my favorite pastimes, but eating locally has brought me back to simplicity. Roasted chicken and veggies, a simple late-summer soup, farm-fresh meatloaf, fruit for dessert, carrots for snacking, fresh herbs for seasoning rather than exotic spices. Cooking with a limited number of fresh ingredients can produce surprisingly delicious results.

5 Stockpile the staples. During downtime from the farm, I'm busy gathering local nuts, oils, vinegars, legumes, and grains. That way, when we get back from our CSA drop in Portland at seven P.M. on a Tuesday in September, it'll be easy to look in the fridge and say, okay the pork chops are thawed and we have some potatoes and lettuce—dinner is panfried pork chops, roasted potatoes with hazelnuts, and a simple oil-and-vinegar-dressed salad.

6 Plan ahead. I'm not a huge fan of meal prep, but spending just a few hours one afternoon a week is worth it to get organized. I hit up the farmers' market and make sure to stock up on veggies, protein, and ingredients that are easy to jazz up our meals with. Bring an iced-down cooler to the market with you so you can keep your goods fresh while you go for an afternoon drive out to a local farm, orchard, dairy, fish market, u-pick berry patch, wild mushroom honeyhole, etc., for weekend recreation. I make it fun—I hit the road on weekends with some of my market goodies and stop along the way at different farm stands and wineries for tastings. I then try to find a beautiful spot to post up for a picnic with my newfound ingredients. On Sunday, I take stock of my market haul and what I've got at home and spend some time planning my meals for the week. Sunday is a good day to cook a big piece of meat or veggie stew for dinner and then have leftovers for a different meal later in the week (chicken salad, pulled pork sandwiches, veggie tacos, pot roast omelet). This is also when I take the time to rehydrate and cook local dried legumes and store them in the fridge for a quick weeknight dinner.

7 Substitutes exist. Like many of us, thanks to Samin Nosrat, I've learned that most successful meals are composed of a balance of salt, fat, acid, and heat. I'm a recipe person, so I keep finding awesome recipes, but these days I look at the ingredients more as food groups,

which allows me to swap in local foods. So, if a recipe calls for coconut oil, I use real butter or a local nut oil. If it calls for halibut, but I have rainbow trout, I try it with rainbow trout. If it calls for cumin and turmeric, I try using a bunch of leafy herbs instead for a pop of flavor. It won't be the same flavor, but it will fulfill the same purpose in the overall dish. I experiment with chopped or dried local hot peppers rather than cracked black pepper for the heat in some of my dishes. I live in wine and orchard country, so I found folks producing local fruit vinegar that I can use instead of lemon juice or rice vinegar. I use a spiralizer to make noodles out of any sturdy vegetable (sweet potatoes, zucchini, regular potatoes, eggplant) for pasta dish recipes. I sub local honey for sugar in my baking recipes and morning coffee.

8 Do it together. I think this is the most important tip. I'm not eating locally alone. I often share meals (simple ones at that) and enjoy the company of good friends and neighbors. I think of eating locally as an opportunity for us all to strengthen our connection to our food, but it's just as much about deepening our bonds with each other.

How to Be a Locavore

Twenty-one foods that can be grown or raised anywhere in the United States:

1. **Eggs** (chicken, duck, quail, goose)
2. **Greens** (kale, spinach, collards, lettuce, bok choy, chard)
3. **Berries** (wild and cultivated)
4. **Root veggies** (carrots, beets, parsnips, turnips, rutabagas)
5. Hot and sweet **peppers**
6. **Meat** (beef, pork, lamb, rabbit)
7. **Poultry** (chicken, duck, turkey)
8. **Tree fruits** (apples and pears in the Pacific Northwest, Midwest, and Northeast; citrus in California and the Southeast; peaches in the Southeast, Northwest, Midwest, and Northeast; mangoes in Hawaii, etc.)
9. **Corn**
10. **Nuts** and **seeds**
11. **Mushrooms** (wild and cultivated)
12. **Onions** and **garlic**
13. **Dairy** products (milk, butter, cheese, yogurt)
14. **Tomatoes**
15. **Wild fish** (salmon, trout, bass, pike, shellfish)
16. **Wild game** (elk, deer, game birds, waterfowl)
17. **Potatoes**
18. **Perennial herbs** (rosemary, thyme, oregano)
19. **Annual herbs** (basil, cilantro, parsley, dill)
20. **Winter** and **summer squash**
21. **Honey**

Essential Recipes for Eating Locally and Well All Year Long

The recipes that follow—for condiments, stocks, sauces, compound butters, and more—add so much flavor to home-cooked meals that I can't imagine my kitchen without them. The recipes throughout the book are pretty minimalist but with just a few additions, like a zesty chimichurri sauce, crushed red pepper flakes, or a basic vinaigrette—you can eat flavorful, fresh, and nourishing meals all year long. Some of these recipes might require one or more "worth the journey" items (page 32), but for the most part, the ingredients should be easy to find in your corner of the world during peak season.

Broth, Stock, and Bone Broth

Bone broth, stock, and broth are nourishing staples I use as a base for soups and stews and to add flavor to so many dishes. They are wonderfully easy and inexpensive to make at home, and they keep for months in the freezer.

What's the difference among the three? Let's start with broth. Broth is the only one that can be completely vegetarian. Broth is typically made with a mix of vegetables, usually onions, carrots, celery—and, if desired, meat (chicken breast, duck legs, turkey thighs, etc.). It's simmered for a short period of time (45 minutes to 2 hours) and is typically seasoned with salt and pepper and sometimes dried herbs. Broth is very light in

**What are the
things that bring
me the most joy
every day?**

flavor, thin in texture, and makes a perfect, unassertive base for soups, stews, and gravies.

I make stock by simmering a combination of animal bones (that still have a little meat left on them) and a mixture of vegetables—usually onions, carrots, and celery—in water. Stock is cooked for anywhere from 2 to 6 hours. Due to its longer cooking time and addition of meat bones, it's higher in nutrition (bones contain protein and lots of vitamins and nutrients, including calcium, magnesium, and phosphorus) and is a good source of collagen. When used as a base for soups, stews, and gravies, it contributes a thicker texture and richer flavor than stock.

Bone broth is made by roasting and then simmering animal bones (chicken, turkey, pork, beef, duck, wild game, etc.), which can have bits of meat still attached or not, anywhere from 12 to 48 hours. It has the lengthiest cook time of the three, which results in a broth that grows more nutrient-dense the longer it cooks, as more collagen-rich gelatin is pulled from the bones. Additionally, a splash of wine or a touch of vinegar can be added to the broth to help dissolve collagen from the bones, producing a silky texture and lovely flavor. Bone broth, which is the richest in flavor of the three, can be sipped on its own straight out of a mug or added to the usual suspects—soups, stews, and gravies.

Homemade stocks, bone broths, and broths are wonderfully nourishing and comforting. If you've ever wondered why chicken soup is prescribed as a cure-all—well, there's science to back it up! Chicken broth has healing powers. It's used as a natural remedy for common colds, flu, and upper respiratory infections because it inhibits neutrophil migration (tongue twister of a term!), which basically means it helps reduce the side effects of those infections.

So with all that knowledge, you can go ahead and make whatever you fancy or have time for. Broth, stock, and bone broth can be used interchangeably throughout this book. You can store the broths and stocks in a jar in the fridge for one week or in the freezer for six months. If you're freezing the jars, be sure to refrigerate them to cool them down before placing them in the freezer (use widemouthed mason jars with one inch of headroom, and this will prevent your jars from cracking). Or you can simply freeze the broth in ice cube trays so you can use smaller amounts as needed.

Basic Bone Broth

MAKES ABOUT
1½ QUARTS

3 pounds bones (chicken, beef, turkey, pork, whatever you've got on hand—either all one kind or a mixture)

2 tablespoons white wine or vinegar

Preheat the oven to 400°F.

Place the bones in a colander, rinse them under cool water, and pat them dry with a kitchen towel.

On a rimmed baking sheet, arrange the bones in a single layer. Roast until they are golden brown, about 30 minutes.

Transfer the hot bones to a stockpot or Dutch oven. Add 3 quarts water and the wine or vinegar and stir to combine. Cover the pot and let it sit for 30 minutes (this will allow the wine or vinegar to extract nutrients from the bones).

Bring the water to a low boil over high heat, then immediately turn the heat down to the lowest setting possible for 24 hours. Check the pot occasionally, skimming off any foam that collects on the surface and adding additional water as needed to keep the ingredients covered.

Strain the broth, discarding the bones.

Pour the broth into mason jars and keep it in the fridge for up to one week or in the freezer for up to six months.

Basic Broth

MAKES ABOUT
1½ QUARTS

Note

To make vegetarian broth, just leave out the meat and bones.

3 pounds assorted meat parts
2 celery stalks with leaves, cut into chunks
2 medium carrots, cut into chunks
2 medium onions, quartered (no need to peel)

2 cloves of garlic, left whole (no need to peel)
2 bay leaves

Place all ingredients in a stockpot or Dutch oven, along with 3 quarts cold water. Slowly bring the mixture to a boil; reduce the heat until it is at a simmer. Simmer, uncovered, for 45 minutes to 2 hours, skimming off any foam as needed and adding additional water as needed to keep the ingredients covered.

Set the meat aside until it is cool enough to handle. Remove the meat from the bones. Discard the bones; save the meat for another use.

Strain the broth, discarding the vegetables and bay leaves.

Pour the broth into mason jars and keep it in the fridge for up to one week or in the freezer for up to six months.

Basic Stock

MAKES ABOUT
1½ QUARTS

Note

The vegetables are added later because cooking them as long as the bones can result in an off flavor.

3 pounds assorted meat bones with a little meat left on, rinsed

2 medium carrots, cut into chunks

2 celery stalks with leaves, cut into chunks

2 cloves of garlic, left whole (no need to peel)

2 medium onions, cut into quarters (no need to peel)

2 bay leaves

Place the bones and 3 quarts of cold water in a stockpot or Dutch oven. Slowly bring the mixture to a boil; reduce the heat until it is at a simmer. Simmer, uncovered, for 45 minutes to 2 hours, skimming foam as needed and adding more water to keep the bones covered as necessary.

Add the vegetables and bay leaves and reduce the heat to a bare simmer (bubbles should just gently break the surface). Cook, skimming frequently, for at least 2 and up to 6 hours. Vegetables are prime at around 3 hours, so feel free to discard the veggies after then or continue to simmer the broth or add them in the final 3 hours.

Strain the broth, discarding the bones, vegetables, and bay leaves.

Pour the broth into mason jars and keep it in the fridge for up to one week or in the freezer for up to six months.

Worth the Journey

Now that we've made local eating a way of life, I do allow myself a handful of nonlocal foods to make cooking our local bounty just a little bit easier (and more pleasurable). The way I determine my "worth the journey" list is simple: First, what are the things that bring me the most joy every day? (Hello, coffee!) Second, what are the things that will easily add flavor to simple dishes like meat, veggies, and salad dressing that I haven't been able to find locally? I always try to keep in mind that triple bottom line of wellness, sustainability, and community when sourcing nonlocal ingredients. I'm sharing my list here in case it is useful, but you will know what items are must-haves for you!

- **Coffee** and **tea**
- **Olive oil**
- **Mustard**
- **Spices** (including salt and pepper)
- **Citrus fruit**
- **Oil-packed anchovies** (which add such a lovely, rich, deep flavor to many recipes)
- **Maple syrup** (You East Coasters are lucky here!)
- Certain **nuts** and **seeds** that may not be local to you
- **Vinegars** (You can find many locally, but an aged balsamic might be harder to find and is a nice treat.)
- **Leavening** (yeast, baking powder, baking soda)
- **Cocoa**
- **Vanilla**
- **Alcohol** (though many parts of the country will have local wine, beer, and spirits)

Chimichurri Sauce

(aka Green Sauce)

MAKES ABOUT
1½ CUPS

I'd double or triple up on this recipe so you can freeze it to keep on hand all winter long. It's a great addition to soups or stews (you'll see I use a dollop or two often throughout this book) and works well on grilled fish, roasted veggies, or as a dip for crackers.

1 cup coarsely chopped parsley
3 tablespoons red wine vinegar
2 large cloves of garlic, minced
½ teaspoon crushed red pepper flakes
Salt and freshly ground black pepper

½ cup extra-virgin olive oil
  (or a natural-tasting nut oil such as
  walnut, hazelnut, or almond),
  plus more to thin as needed

Combine all ingredients in a food processor and blend until well integrated. Add more oil to thin as needed. Taste for seasonings and adjust as needed.

Classic Mayo

MAKES ABOUT
1½ CUPS

Note
To make a fun aioli, add a garlic clove or two, or stir in some chili powder and lime juice for a spicy kick!

This classic condiment is just the thing to make any sandwich or salad a little bit more decadent. From my experience, homemade mayo simply cannot be beat. The texture and flavor are top-notch, and because it's fresher and more flavorful than store-bought, a little bit goes a long way.

1 large egg yolk
½ teaspoon Dijon mustard
½ teaspoon salt
1 tablespoon white wine vinegar
  or lemon juice

1¼ cups light olive oil or another
  light-tasting oil (like grapeseed,
  sunflower, or safflower oil)

In the bowl of a food processor or blender, place the yolk, mustard, salt, and vinegar. Pulse until the ingredients are well combined.

While the food processor or blender is running, slowly (very slowly) drizzle in the oil. When an emulsion forms, you can add the oil a little faster. Taste test and adjust seasonings as needed.

Store the mayo in an airtight container or mason jar in the fridge for up to seven days.

Herb Butter

MAKES ABOUT
½ CUP BUTTER

I love making this compound butter throughout the summer with different herbs, and even sometimes go wild, swapping out the savory flavorings for fresh lavender and honey. This is a forgiving recipe, so have fun with it! It keeps well in the freezer all year long.

½ cup (1 stick) unsalted butter, softened to room temperature

¼ cup minced mixed herbs (such as basil, thyme, parsley, dill, or chives)

½ clove of garlic, smashed

1 teaspoon coarse sea salt

1 teaspoon freshly ground black pepper

In a small bowl, combine all the ingredients. Mix well until the herbs are distributed evenly. Taste for seasoning and adjust as needed.

Scoop the mixture out onto a piece of waxed or parchment paper. Shape it into a cylinder or disk, and seal the ends by twisting. Alternatively, pack it into a mason jar and secure it with a lid. Chill it in the refrigerator until firm, at least an hour.

Will keep in the refrigerator for about a month and in the freezer for up to six months.

Zucchini Butter

MAKES ABOUT
2 CUPS

This buttery spread is the condiment you never knew you needed! It tastes great on toast, spreads well on pizza dough, adds flavor to grilled eggplant rounds, and spoons perfectly into savory oatmeal with a fried egg in the morning. It's also a wonderful way to use up the abundance of zucchini throughout the summer months. I like to stir in a touch of ground sumac, which is generally an imported spice, but you can substitute a little freshly grated lemon zest or a tiny dash of white wine vinegar.

2 pounds zucchini or assorted
   summer squash
¼ cup unsalted butter
2 cloves of garlic, minced
1 teaspoon dried thyme

½ teaspoon sumac (optional but
   adds a bright zesty note)
Salt and freshly ground black pepper
Water or white wine if needed to
   deglaze the pan

With a box grater or with the grating attachment on your food processor, coarsely grate the zucchini. Wring out most of the liquid from the zucchini with a dish towel.

Place the butter in a medium-sized deep cast-iron pan over medium-high heat. Once the butter starts to melt, add the garlic, thyme, sumac (if using), grated zucchini, and salt and pepper to taste. Cook, stirring often, until the zucchini reaches a spreadable consistency, 15 to 18 minutes. The mixture will still have plenty of texture but will be more jamlike after cooking. If you scorch the bottom of the mixture, turn the flame down, but don't stress! Just stir those crispy burnt bits into the butter for added flavor! If need be, add a touch of water or white wine to deglaze the pan. The zucchini will hold its bright green color and slowly caramelize into a nice vegetable jam.

Store the butter in a glass jar in the fridge for up to two weeks.

Simple Vinaigrette

MAKES ABOUT
½ CUP

When making vinaigrette, I use a 1:4 ratio (one part vinegar to four parts oil). Sometimes I use raspberry vinegar and hazelnut oil for a simple salad dressing or marinade. Other times it's great to jazz things up with a pumpkin seed oil, fresh (or dried) minced sage, and some balsamic vinegar for a richer dressing that goes well with heartier greens (like kale, spinach, beet greens, and collards). Regardless, whether you decide to use local oils and vinegars or to purchase them from the store, remember, quality is everything.

2 tablespoons vinegar of your choice
Pinch each of salt and freshly ground
  black pepper

8 tablespoons olive oil

In a small mason jar or bowl, combine the vinegar, salt, and pepper. Give it a good stir, then drizzle in the oil. Secure the lid and shake until the oil is mixed in and the dressing tastes just right.

Store the dressing in an airtight container in the fridge for up to seven days.

Herb Goat Cheese Dressing

MAKES ABOUT
½ CUP

I love this tangy dressing that combines goat cheese and buttermilk for the perfect level of creaminess. You can make it year-round using dried herbs, but in the heart of spring and summer, nothing beats the bright flavor of fresh herbs.

4 ounces goat cheese, at room
  temperature
2 tablespoons buttermilk
1 teaspoon dried parsley
¼ teaspoon dried dill

2 teaspoons red wine vinegar
2 tablespoons olive oil
Pinch of salt and freshly ground black
  pepper

Place all the ingredients in a blender (or use an immersion blender) and blend until smooth and creamy. Taste for seasonings and adjust as needed.

Store the dressing in an airtight container in the fridge for up to seven days.

Honey Ketchup

MAKES ABOUT
2½ CUPS

I'm sorry, folks, this isn't Heinz ketchup—but I promise you, it's absolutely delicious! I love using local honey as the sweetener and adding a touch of warming spices (I find they really tie the flavors together), but feel free to leave them out if you prefer a more traditional ketchup.

12 ounces tomato paste (page 39)
⅓ cup plus 1 tablespoon honey
¾ cup apple cider vinegar
2 teaspoons salt

¼ teaspoon garlic powder
¼ teaspoon ground allspice
¼ teaspoon ground cinnamon

In a saucepan, mix together all the ingredients, along with ½ cup water, using a wooden spoon.

Bring the mixture to a boil, then reduce the heat to low and partially cover the pan (it will spit hot tomato sauce). Simmer 15 to 20 minutes, stirring occasionally. If it seems too thick, add a touch of water, until you reach your desired ketchup consistency.

Let the mixture cool completely.

Pour the ketchup into a mason jar and keep refrigerated for up to a month. If it thickens too much in the fridge, add a little water to get it to a pourable consistency.

Tomato Paste

MAKES ABOUT 20
OUNCES OF PASTE

Note

If your tomatoes were extra juicy and won't fit onto the rimmed baking sheets after you press them through the food mill, feel free to simmer the tomato puree on the stovetop before placing it in the oven. You can reduce the mixture by up to a third or by half. Then pour this more concentrated tomato mixture onto the rimmed baking sheets to finish reducing in the oven.

Tomato paste is a highly concentrated ingredient that is full of tomato flavor and adds so much richness and depth to recipes that a little bit goes a long way. To make tomato paste, any mix of tomatoes will work: heirlooms, hybrids, and even cherry tomatoes, though romas have the least amount of moisture, so the cooking time will be shorter.

10 pounds tomatoes
  (any mix will work)
2 tablespoons olive oil, plus more
  for topping the jars

2 teaspoons sea salt

Preheat the oven to 300°F and arrange two racks to divide the oven into thirds.

With a sharp knife, quarter the tomatoes (if you're using cherry tomatoes, leave them whole).

Heat the olive oil in a large pot over medium-high heat. Add the tomatoes and cook until they are softened and the skins begin to detach from the flesh.

Use a wooden spoon to push the tomatoes through a food mill or fine-mesh sieve to separate the tomato pulp from the seeds and skins. Stir in the salt. Discard or compost the seeds and skins.

Divide the tomato pulp between two rimmed baking sheets (see note). Bake the tomato pulp until reduced to a thick paste. This will take anywhere from 3 to 4 hours (note that baking times will depend on the ripeness and juiciness of your tomatoes). Check the tomatoes every half hour, stirring the paste and scraping up any caramelized bits to incorporate them into the mixture, and switching the position of the baking sheets so that they reduce evenly.

Remove the baking sheets from the oven and let the paste cool.

Transfer the paste into 4-ounce jars and drizzle a touch of olive oil on top before securing the lid. You can also divide the paste between individual ice cube trays for individual portions. Refrigerate it for up to three weeks or freeze it for up to nine months.

Honey Simple Syrup

**MAKES ABOUT
1½ CUPS**

I get so jealous of my East Coast friends who have access to local maple syrup! However, honey is available across the United States, and this simple syrup is delicious and easy to mix into salad dressings, cocktails, baked goods, or a cup of hot coffee or tea. You can also drizzle it over yogurt or ice cream. Feel free to get creative and add a vanilla bean, thyme sprigs, rosemary (or any fresh herb, really). Cardamom pods and cinnamon sticks make for a spicy, warm, festive honey in the fall.

1 cup honey   Spices or herbs to taste (optional)

In a medium-sized saucepan over medium heat, stir together honey, herbs or spices, and 1 cup water until the honey dissolves. Increase the heat slightly, then simmer for 5 to 7 minutes, stirring often.

Let the mixture cool to room temperature and discard any spices or herbs if using.

Pour the syrup into a mason jar and refrigerate it for up to a month.

How to Dry and Preserve Fresh Herbs

Drying fresh herbs is an easy and inexpensive way to enjoy them all year long. Homemade dried herbs are also generally more pungent than grocery store herbs—you'll find you don't need to add as much to your recipes to give that added kick. You can dry herbs in a variety of different ways; hang-drying, oven-drying, and the use of a home dehydrator are all great options.

I've learned that it's important to harvest herbs at the right time—they should be picked before the flowers develop (which can cause them to become bitter). It's best to prepare one variety of herb for drying at a time, as you don't want the aromas to mix.

Begin by discarding any dead or limp leaves. Strip large-leaved herbs, such as sage, parsley, basil, and mint, from their stalks. Leave small-leaved herbs, like dill, thyme, rosemary, and oregano, on the stalks until drying is complete.

The trick for effective drying is to expose the herbs to dry, fresh air. A well-ventilated, warm place out of direct sunlight is ideal. If you live in a humid area, the process may be slower, and mold can be a problem. If that's the case, a home dehydrator or your oven will be the best option. Models vary, so I recommend following the manufacturer's instructions when using a dehydrator.

Directions for hang-drying herbs

1. **Tie sprigs or branches** into small bunches. Smaller bunches are better than large ones because air can circulate more evenly.

2. **Hang the bunches**, leaves pointing downward, on an herb-drying rack or even a wire closet hanger. Wrap the herbs loosely in muslin or a thin paper bag with a few tiny holes poked in it to keep out dust and to catch falling leaves or seeds. Do not use plastic bags, because mold can develop easily.

3. **Dry them** for seven to ten days. The herbs are ready when they're flaky and easy to crush. To store, crumble the herbs with your fingers and place them in small airtight containers.

For oven-drying
(one of my favorite methods because it's the fastest and easiest!)

1. **Space out the leaves** or small branches (like thyme and rosemary) on a baking sheet and place in an oven set to the lowest possible temperature. Leave the door ajar to allow moisture to escape.

2. **Turn the leaves over** after 15 minutes to ensure even drying; they will be quite dry after about an hour. Turn off the oven and leave the herbs in there until they are completely cool.

3. **Crumble** the dried herbs with your fingers (discard the woody stems) and store them in small airtight containers.

How to Make Crushed Red Pepper Flakes

I put crushed red pepper flakes on EVERYTHING. Seriously, I have a problem. Eggs, roasted veggies, pizza, pasta, soups, even in some desserts! I'll admit that sometimes I go so crazy with overseasoning my food, but what can I say? I like a little heat.

We grow a lot of cayenne peppers at our farm, and I think they make the best crushed red pepper flakes. However, you can use any type of hot pepper. If you want to make them extra hot, try mixing in some habanero or ghost peppers. Or make green pepper flakes using jalapeños and serranos. My favorite method for drying peppers is to pop them in the oven, but you can also hang-dry them. They take longer than herbs to completely dry out (usually three or four weeks) but you can use the same basic method (though you want to make sure to give peppers a bit more room between each other than herbs).

Directions for oven-drying peppers

1 With a gloved hand, cut off and discard the tops, then spread the peppers out on a dry baking sheet. Place them in the oven at its lowest temperature (180 or 200°F) and leave the door ajar to let moisture escape. Dry for 2–3 hours or until no moisture is left and the peppers are brittle and break apart easily. If they're still soft, then put them back into the oven.

2 Keep an eye on the peppers during the final hour, as you can easily overdo it. I've overcooked a few batches, and while they're still fine once crushed, they're not nearly as tasty as perfectly done peppers. Cooking time will vary from kitchen to kitchen, and you'll start to perfect your method the more you do it.

3 Once the peppers are dried and cooled to room temperature, use a mini food processor or blender to crush them. Store them in a small airtight container. They will keep for up to a year, but their potency will die down a bit after about six months.

Sourdough Bread

MAKES 2 LOAVES

There is nothing more humble, satisfying, or comforting than a slice of sourdough bread fresh from the oven. Sourdough is unique because it doesn't require commercial yeast to rise. It's made with a live fermented culture of flour, water, sourdough starter—which acts as a natural leavening agent—and salt. Sourdough is known for its unique, slightly sour flavor, chewy texture, and crisp crust. Due to its long fermentation, it trumps store-bought loaves when it comes to health. It's easier to digest, makes your house smell amazing, and is damn delicious!

This recipe comes straight from the kitchen of our favorite local bakery. Sourdough really is a touch-and-feel kind of process. In all honesty, it took me a few trials and errors to get the method down. I would recommend following this recipe but also checking out some YouTube videos on how to do the stretch-and-fold method. You can make your own sourdough starter, or ask your local bakery if you can purchase a little of theirs. To make your own starter, you need only two ingredients: flour and water.

Jure, the bread baker who taught me this method, instilled this very important message in me: Baking sourdough bread is more than just a recipe. . . . It's an understanding.

You'll notice that there are similar recipes out there, and yet no two loaves look alike. The process is all about timing and personal touch. Once you've spent some time with this recipe, the process becomes a natural rhythm, and in the end, you will have created your very own unique bread. With some patience, practice, good-quality butter, and salt, you're on your way to a life-changing experience!

EQUIPMENT

- Sourdough starter
- Mixing bowl
- Small kitchen scale (For most bakers, a digital scale is one of the most beloved and reliable kitchen tools. The results of the finished product are consistent and dependable. And a scale is inexpensive, doesn't take up much room, and is a great thing to have on hand if you want to use more local ingredients that don't always come premeasured. Think butter from your local dairy, a jar of milk, yogurt, or bulk grains. A scale is a great addition to your kitchen!)
- 2 proofing baskets (Proofing baskets support the shaped loaves during their final rise before baking. You can buy the same kind of wicker proofing baskets that bakers use, or you can simply use mixing bowls.)
- 2 small rags or terry cloths for the proofing baskets
- 2 kitchen towels to cover the dough while rising, plus more for handling the dough
- Bench knife or a large sharp knife (Bench knives are ideal for cutting dough and can be found at any kitchen store or online.)
- Serrated knife or blade to score the top of the dough
- Dutch oven

INGREDIENTS

900 grams high-gluten flour (aka bread flour)
  or all-purpose flour
100 grams whole wheat flour
100 grams sourdough starter
750 grams water
20 grams salt

In a large bowl, mix the flours, sourdough starter, and water.

Let the mixture rest for at least 20 minutes and up to 2 hours.

Add the salt by mixing and folding the dough. Simply gather a portion of the dough, stretch it upward, and then fold it over itself. Rotate the bowl a quarter turn and repeat this process until you have come full circle.

Cover the dough with a kitchen towel and store it at warm room temperature (75 to 85°F) for 90 minutes to 2 hours.

Uncover and fold the dough every 30 minutes. To do this, dip your hands in water and stretch the dough upward and then fold one side over; repeat on the other three sides.

After three turns and roughly 2 hours, place the dough on a lightly floured counter and cut it in half using the bench knife or a large sharp knife.

Shape the dough into balls and let them rest for 20 to 30 minutes.

For the final shaping, after the dough has relaxed, shape each piece into a ball using the stretch-and-fold method. Liberally coat two kitchen cloths with flour—use more flour than you think you need and really rub it in with your fingers. Line each proofing basket with a flour-coated cloth. Transfer the dough balls into the lined bread baskets and cover each with a kitchen towel.

Let the dough rise at room temperature for 3 to 5 hours or overnight in the refrigerator.

To bake: Preheat the oven to 500°F. Place the Dutch oven, covered, in the oven for 20 minutes of the preheating time. When you're ready to bake, carefully remove the Dutch oven, take off the lid, and tip a dough ball into the pot seam side down. Score the top with a serrated knife or razor blade. Replace the lid and return the pot to the oven.

Bake for 20 minutes at 500°F. Turn the oven down to 450°F and remove the lid (careful, hot steam will come out). Bake uncovered for another 20 to 30 minutes, until the crust is a deep golden brown. Return the oven temperature to 500°F and repeat with the second loaf.

Cool the loaves and enjoy.

How to make bread crumbs

Homemade bread crumbs are easy to prepare and so much better than store-bought, which are usually stale and lack flavor and texture. I keep a stash of bread crumbs on hand all the time to add crunch and texture to salads or roasted vegetables. I also sprinkle them on soups and macaroni and cheese (page 124), and add them to meatloaf.

Here's how to make them: Preheat the oven to 300°F. Place slices of sourdough bread (or any type of hearty bread) on a baking sheet and dry them out slightly in the oven for 15 minutes. Let the bread cool a bit before pulsing it in a food processor or blender. Make sure to add the bread in small batches for best results and uniform size. I like my crumbs to be about the size of grains of rice.

Store them in a mason jar in the refrigerator for up to one month or in the freezer for up to three months.

Baking sourdough bread is more than just a recipe. . . . It's an understanding.

Sourdough Starter

If you aren't one of the lucky ones to get a 100-year-old starter (usually accompanied with a name like Thelma or Barbra) passed down to you, you're not alone and you can still make your own sourdough bread! The great news is that you only need two ingredients to create your sourdough starter: flour and water. The process takes anywhere from 5 to 7 days to get the wild yeast to grow strong enough to make your first loaf. The temperature of your kitchen will dictate how fast or slow your starter will activate. A warmer kitchen will be faster, while a cooler kitchen will take a bit more time. The ideal temperature is 70°–75°. Each day you'll "feed" your starter with equal parts flour and water. You'll begin to notice after a few days that the mixture will start to bubble a bit and smell slightly sour. This is a great sign! Now you're halfway to making your first loaf of homemade bread!

100 grams all-purpose flour   100 grams water

In a large, widemouthed mason jar or medium-sized glass bowl (avoid metal), mix the flour and water vigorously with a wooden spoon. Seal the top with plastic wrap or with a dish towel secured with a rubber band and set aside on the counter for 24 hours.

The next day, discard half the batter (which you can compost) and add equal parts flour and water (you need only about 60 grams of each for every feeding). Give the mixture a good stir and secure the jar or bowl with plastic wrap or a dish towel and set aside for another 24 hours.

Repeat this process until your starter looks bubbly and has a slightly sour smell (anywhere from 3 to 6 days). You can test your starter to see if it's active enough by dropping a small amount of it into a bowl of room-temperature water. If it floats, it's active enough; if it sinks, you will need to keep feeding it for another day or two. As you get comfortable making sourdough bread weekly, you can keep your starter going yearlong. However, if you don't plan to bake for a while, you can place your starter in the fridge for months. Just remember, it will take a bit longer to activate once it's been chilled.

Farm Stand Freezer Tomato Sauce

MAKES APPROXIMATELY
5 CUPS SAUCE

When the middle of winter hits, this is the staple I thank myself most for having taken the time to prepare. Opening up a jar of vibrant tomato sauce from the peak of the summer is pure bliss when it's snowing outside!

¼ cup unsalted butter
2 large onions, diced
5 cloves of garlic, minced
9 cups chopped tomatoes
   (A mix of heirlooms and round
   reds is great here.)

1 pint cherry tomatoes
1 cup dry red wine
2 teaspoons dried oregano
¾ cup basil leaves, chopped
Fine sea salt and freshly ground
   black pepper

In a large saucepan over medium heat, melt the butter. Add the onions and cook until tender, about 6 minutes. Add the garlic and cook for 2 minutes longer. Stir in the tomatoes, red wine, oregano, and basil. Season with lots of salt and pepper.

Cook the sauce for about 30 minutes, stirring occasionally. Then reduce the heat to low and simmer for 3 to 4 hours or until thickened. Taste for seasonings and adjust as needed.

Remove the saucepan from the heat and use an immersion blender (or a regular blender) to puree the sauce or a potato masher to break it up. (If you like it on the thicker side with some texture, use the potato masher; if you like it smooth and creamy, use a blender.)

Let the sauce cool to room temperature.

Ladle the sauce into widemouthed mason jars, making sure to leave at least 2 inches of headspace. Place them in the fridge for 8 hours before transferring them to the freezer. These steps help ensure the jars won't crack when frozen.

Store the sauce in the freezer for up to six months and use it for all your favorite tomato sauce dishes!

Oregon Hazelnut Pesto

MAKES ABOUT
1½ CUPS

I put this pesto on everything—eggs, pasta, veggies, you name it. If you live outside the Pacific Northwest, feel free to substitute any nut or seed for the hazelnuts. The flavor will be different but still delicious! The pesto freezes well, so I encourage you to make a double or triple batch.

½ cup hazelnuts
2 to 3 large cloves of garlic
2 cups packed fresh basil leaves
¾ cup olive oil, plus more for
  topping the jars

Salt
Red wine vinegar

In a small skillet over medium heat, toast the hazelnuts, shaking the pan often, until they are fragrant and lightly browned, about 8 minutes.

Remove the pan from the heat. When the nuts are cool enough to handle, roll them in a kitchen towel to remove the skins. (You don't have to be perfect here, some of the skins are fine left on.)

Return the skillet to medium heat and add the garlic cloves. Toast the garlic until lightly browned on all sides, 4 to 6 minutes, making sure to shake the pan often to ensure you don't burn them.

Add the hazelnuts, garlic, and basil leaves to the bowl of a food processor. Process until a coarse texture is achieved. With the motor running, slowly drizzle in the olive oil. Season with plenty of salt and a splash of red wine vinegar. Continue to process until everything is well blended. Taste for seasonings and adjust as needed.

Fill a widemouthed pint or two half-pint mason jars with the pesto, leaving at least 1 inch of headspace. Drizzle with a little oil and seal. The pesto will keep in the freezer for up to 6 months.

Fall

Fall, also known as harvest season. The leaves are turning, burn piles are being lit, animals are going off to slaughter, farmers are hauling thousands of pounds of winter squash out of their fields. There is a new (and oftentimes welcome) chill in the air. The mornings tend to be crisp, the sun rises a little later, and long sleeves and heavy boots get pulled out and dusted off. Warm mugs of coffee and tea are savored as the sun slowly lights up the morning sky.

The first real frost of October will take with it any remaining zucchini, tomatoes, and eggplants, but that same freeze sweetens up the carrots, parsnips, broccoli, and kale. Fall is one of the most celebrated seasons for eating, because dwindling summer crops overlap with the heartier fall bounty. A late-summer corn chowder can be served warm, enjoyed with a side of sautéed collard greens and a hunk of fresh bread—because it's cool enough to want warm food, to turn on the oven again. It is really a special time of year, and we revel in the change of season.

On a Friday evening in late October, long after our field crew has gone home for the day and the last of the evening farm chores are complete, Taylor and I crack open a bottle of Syrah gifted to us from our friend and fellow farmer James Mantone. It's his own wine, made with grapes grown on his farm just across the river from Tumbleweed. I can still taste the first sip warming my throat as I start chopping onions that spent the better part of the late summer curing in the barn. And while I chop and mince, Taylor browns meat from our friends Tim and Keely Jefferies's ranch. It's a cold evening, and we're hungry for comfort—so, Beef and Rutabaga Stew is on the menu. Once all our ingredients are prepped, we let the stew simmer for a while and sit back next to the woodstove with our glasses of wine, still wearing our dirty work clothes, and allow the warmth from the fire and wine to settle into our bodies. It's not even six P.M., and while most of our friends are getting ready to head out for a night at the pub, we relish the quiet, simple pleasure of staying in. Even if we wanted to join our friends,

There's beauty in slowing down and recognizing these small feats.

we wouldn't last long. Saturday mornings, the alarm clock goes off at four so we can load the trailer for the weekend farmers' market. Saturday is our longest and most stressful day of the week, so for seven months out of the year (when the Saturday market is open to the public), Friday evenings are typically spent in this fashion. Home-cooked dinner, messy kitchen, tasty wine, and lights out by eight P.M.

Our farm has come a long way in the seven years since we branched out on our own, away from the only farm we knew and the farmers who gave us our great education. We started off small, feeding only a handful of neighbors (and very gracious family members who joined our CSA). And seven years later, our farm can now feed hundreds of people from the three and a half acres we cultivate. Our farm is six acres, but as we've gotten smarter and more efficient with our growing practices, we've actually shrunk our field space and grow more food on less acreage. Our CSA no longer comprises only generous family members; we now have a healthy wait list, and our farmers' market booth is flourishing with beautiful produce that we are proud to call our own.

The fertility of our fields comes from local compost, tilled-in cover crops, and manure from our pigs and chickens. It's taken years to get this kind of nutrition into our soil, but it's beautiful to see the difference in the quality of our vegetables year after year. We love seeing our produce highlighted on the menus of local restaurants, and the relationships we've cultivated with the wonderful chefs have been an important part of our business. It's usually on these crisp fall evenings, as we sip our wine and patiently wait for our stew to slowly cook, that we're reminded of how far we've come and how grateful we are to do what we love and to share it with our community. There's beauty in slowing down and recognizing these small feats, and autumn offers the opportunity for reflection and gratitude. Our farm has demanded more from us than we ever could have imagined. And we've given it everything; our physical strength, our mental and emotional reserves. Just when we think we have nothing left to give, the farm gives back.

While fall is a great time of year to take a moment for reflection, for us, it's also the season of preparation. It's when we take advantage of the waning daylight to stock up for the winter ahead. I spend a lot of my time preserving our summer bounty—freezing vegetables, making fruit preserves, canning pumpkin puree. As the days grow shorter and darker, people are also looking to connect and gather. We spend our weekends inside with friends and neighbors, sharing the work of chopping, mincing, and boiling for canning; drying herbs; making batches of compound butter. We check our freezer to make sure it's working properly because we will rely on it to feed us all winter long. Once it's fully stocked, we can relax, safe in the knowledge that our hard work will allow us to eat like kings.

Pumpkin-
Hazelnut
Honey Bread

MAKES 1 LOAF

Localize it

Swap out pumpkin puree for any winter squash puree (acorn, delicata, butternut). Use any nut or seed oil (walnut, pumpkin seed, grapeseed, sunflower, or even olive oil). Try maple syrup instead of honey if you can get it locally. Walnuts, almonds, pecans, or pumpkin seeds will all work well in place of the hazelnuts.

When we first decided to go local, I was afraid I'd miss out on baking, but I quickly found that there were so many lovely local ingredients I could use to satisfy my sweet tooth. On the first chilly mornings of autumn, there is absolutely nothing more comforting than a thick slice of this sweet, spicy pumpkin loaf.

⅓ cup hazelnut oil, plus additional for greasing the pan
½ cup honey
2 large eggs
1 cup pumpkin puree (Homemade is best here; see note.)
¼ cup whole milk

1 teaspoon ground cinnamon
½ teaspoon freshly grated nutmeg
1 teaspoon baking soda
1 teaspoon vanilla extract
½ teaspoon salt
1 cup whole wheat flour
¾ cup all-purpose flour
½ cup chopped hazelnuts

Preheat the oven to 325°F and grease a 9-by-5-inch loaf pan with oil.

In a large bowl, beat the oil and honey together with a whisk. Add the eggs and whisk until blended.

Add the pumpkin puree, milk, cinnamon, nutmeg, baking soda, vanilla, and salt and whisk to blend.

With a wooden spoon, stir in the flours just until combined. Some lumps are okay!

Pour the batter into the greased loaf pan and sprinkle with the chopped hazelnuts.

Bake for 50 to 55 minutes or until a toothpick inserted into the center comes out clean.

Let the bread cool in the pan for 10 minutes, then carefully transfer the loaf to a wire rack to cool for 20 minutes before slicing.

Note

To make pumpkin puree, simply slice a 3- to 4-pound sugar pumpkin (or any winter squash) in half. Scoop out the seeds and fiber with a large spoon. Reserve the seeds for another use. Lay the pumpkin cut side down on a parchment- or silicone-lined baking sheet. Roast it in a 400°F oven until it is tender and easily pierced with a fork, 40 to 45 minutes. When the halves are cool enough to handle, scoop the flesh into the bowl of a food processor—or use a wooden spoon to beat by hand—and process until smooth, scraping down the sides of your processor as needed. Store the puree in jars or Tupperware in the fridge for up to seven days or freeze it for up to six months.

Pork Chops with Cranberry-Port Sauce

SERVES 4

Localize it

Try any full-bodied red wine for the port, but add a little honey if you do. Try substituting frozen blueberries, raspberries, or blackberries for the fresh cranberries (thaw them before using). I imagine this sauce would also be delicious with steak or duck.

This is my favorite way to serve pork chops, and with the abundance of cranberries and fresh-pressed apple cider available in the fall, this is one local recipe that couldn't be easier to pull off. Pair it with a glass of your favorite red wine or hard cider, and you've got yourself a lovely dinner.

FOR THE CRANBERRY-PORT SAUCE
1 cup ruby port
2 cinnamon sticks, broken in half
⅛ teaspoon ground cloves
1 (12-ounce) bag fresh cranberries
¾ cup apple cider
¼ cup honey, or more to taste
Fine sea salt

FOR THE PORK CHOPS
4 (1-inch-thick) bone-in pork chops
Salt and freshly ground black pepper
1 teaspoon minced thyme
2 tablespoons unsalted butter

Make the sauce: In a medium-sized pot, bring the ruby port, cinnamon sticks, and ground cloves to a boil. Reduce the heat to medium and simmer for about 5 minutes.

Add the cranberries, apple cider, and honey. Bring to a boil, stirring often, until the honey dissolves. Reduce the heat to medium-low, cover the pot, and simmer until the sauce has thickened and most of the cranberries have collapsed, 15 to 20 minutes. Stir often so the berries don't burn on the bottom of the pan. Add a hefty pinch of salt and taste for seasoning. If the sauce doesn't seem sweet enough, add a bit more honey.

Make the pork chops: Sprinkle the pork chops with salt, pepper, and minced thyme.

In a heavy-bottom pan, over medium-high heat, melt the butter until it's beginning to brown a bit. Add the pork chops and cook until they are browned and cooked through, or until an instant-read thermometer inserted into the thickest part of the pork reads 145°F, 5 to 6 minutes per side. (Note that the chops will continue to cook briefly when they are taken off the heat.)

Plate the pork chops and spoon a little cranberry port sauce over each. Serve with additional sauce on the side.

Pumpkin Pot Pie with Sausage and Kale

SERVES 6

Localize it

Try ground chicken or turkey for the pork. Any variety of winter squash will work beautifully here. Don't have kale? Spinach, chard, collard greens, or even turnip greens will work just fine.

When I made this recipe for our CSA members, I received a flood of emails unlike any I'd read before! Folks just really loved it, and I don't blame them. The fall and winter are a great time to whip up pot pies. (You can get creative with the filling and use whatever ingredients you have on hand!) This version is absolutely delicious and a great way to celebrate the fall harvest.

FOR THE CRUST
½ cup (1 stick) cold unsalted butter
1¼ cups all-purpose flour (spooned and leveled), plus more for the work surface
¼ teaspoon fine sea salt
3 to 5 tablespoons ice water

FOR THE FILLING AND ASSEMBLY
1 pound ground pork
1 large onion, finely chopped
1½ teaspoons dried sage
Pinch of freshly grated nutmeg

Hefty pinch each of salt and freshly ground black pepper
1 small bunch of kale, tough stems discarded, coarsely chopped
1 small to medium sugar pie pumpkin, seeded and cut into ½-inch cubes (no need to peel), for a total of about 1½ cups
¼ cup all-purpose flour
3 cups homemade or low-sodium chicken or pork stock (page 31)
1 egg
2 tablespoons cream or milk

Preheat the oven to 375°F.

Make the crust: Cube the cold butter into ½-inch dice with a sharp knife and place it in the freezer to cool back down after handling. In a food processor, pulse together the flour and salt. Add the cubed butter and pulse 12 to 16 times or until the mixture resembles coarse meal, with a few pea-sized pieces of butter remaining. With the machine running, gently pour in 3 tablespoons of the water. Pulse until the dough begins to form a ball (it may still be crumbly, and that's okay as long as when you pinch it, the mixture holds together). If it seems too dry, add a touch more ice water. Do not overmix.

Form the dough into a disk, wrap it tightly in plastic, and refrigerate until firm, 45 minutes to 1 hour. (You can also leave the dough in the fridge overnight, or freeze it for up to a month.)

Make the filling: In a large, deep cast-iron pot over medium-high heat, cook the pork, using a wooden spoon to break up the meat a bit. Cook until it is lightly browned and no longer pink. Transfer the pork to a paper-towel-lined plate to drain. Add the onion, sage, nutmeg, salt, and pepper to the pot. Cook, stirring occasionally, for about 5 minutes. Add the kale and pumpkin and cook until the pumpkin begins to soften, about 5 minutes.

Sprinkle in the flour and stir well. Slowly add the stock, ½ cup at a time. Bring the mixture to a boil, reduce the heat, and simmer until the pumpkin softens and the mixture thickens up a bit, 8 to 10 minutes. Return the pork to the pot and give it a good stir. Remove the pot from the heat.

In a small bowl, make an egg wash by whisking the egg with the cream or milk. Then, on a floured work surface, roll out the dough to ⅛-inch thickness. Place the dough over the pot (being careful not to burn yourself) and fold the overhang inward while pinching to crimp the edge. Alternatively, you can transfer the filling to a pie pan and drape the crust over the pie pan (if you have leftover filling, save it for breakfast the next day and top it with a fried egg). Cut vents in the dough. Brush with the egg wash.

Place the dish on a rimmed baking sheet and bake until the crust is golden brown and the filling is bubbling around the edges, 45 to 50 minutes.

Transfer the pot pie to a wire rack and let cool for 15 minutes before serving.

Buttermilk Biscuits with Honey Butter

MAKES 8 TO 10
BISCUITS

Localize it

Swap in maple syrup for honey. A mix of whole wheat and all-purpose flour will yield a denser biscuit but will be equally delicious.

This recipe was passed down to me in the "recipe book" my mother-in-law made me as a wedding present. The recipes were from friends, mothers, grandmothers, aunts, and neighbors. I'm not sure who contributed this one, but I've made these biscuits for years without fail.

FOR THE BISCUITS
2½ cups all-purpose flour
2 tablespoons baking powder
1 teaspoon salt
½ cup (1 stick) cold unsalted butter, cubed
1 cup plus 2 tablespoons cold buttermilk
2 teaspoons honey

FOR THE HONEY BUTTER
½ cup (1 stick) unsalted butter, softened
2 tablespoons honey
Flaky sea salt to taste

Preheat the oven to 425°F.

In a large bowl, whisk the flour, baking powder, and salt until combined. Add the cubed butter and cut it into the dry ingredients with a pastry cutter or two knives until the mixture is coarse and pebbly.

Make a well in the center of the mixture. Pour 1 cup of the buttermilk on top, then drizzle in the honey. Stir everything together until it is combined, being careful to not overwork the dough. It will be very crumbly, and that's okay.

Gather the dough into a ball. On a lightly floured surface, press it into a rough 8-inch square (it doesn't have to be perfect). Fold it in thirds like a letter. Turn the dough 90 degrees and fold it in thirds again, forming a small square. Press or roll the dough back into an 8-inch square and repeat once, adding flour as needed to prevent sticking.

Gently roll the dough out with a rolling pin until it's about ½ inch thick. Cut it into 3-inch circles. (A mason jar is perfect for this!) Reroll any scraps until you have 8 to 10 biscuits.

In a 10-inch cast-iron skillet or on a baking sheet, arrange the biscuits close together. (When they are close together, even touching, they rise better!)

Brush the tops with the remaining 2 tablespoons of buttermilk. Bake the biscuits for 15 minutes or until the tops are golden brown.

Meanwhile, make the honey butter: In a medium bowl, stir the butter and honey until well combined. Top with a sprinkling of flaky sea salt to taste.

Serve the biscuits warm with the honey butter.

Marinated Beet and Bread Salad with Fresh Herbs and Goat Cheese

SERVES 4

Localize it

This would be great served with any variety of beets or even sweet potato, pumpkin, or butternut squash. If you go with the sweet potato or squash, I'd try using sage or parsley as the herb of choice.

This salad is an absolutely divine way to prepare and serve beets as the star of the show. It's hearty enough to be enjoyed as a main course, but I suggest serving it alongside roasted chicken (page 211) or steak for a complete dinner.

1½ pounds beets, sliced into
  ½-inch pieces (no need to peel)
Salt
1 small red onion, thinly sliced
¼ cup balsamic vinegar
2 teaspoons honey
6 tablespoons olive oil,
  plus more for drizzling
Freshly ground black pepper
½ loaf sourdough bread (page 44),
  torn into 1-inch pieces
  (about 6 cups)
4 ounces goat cheese, crumbled
1 cup torn fresh herbs
  (dill, parsley, basil)

Preheat the oven to 425°F.

Place the beets in a large pot with enough water to cover them by at least 1 inch. Sprinkle them with a hefty pinch of salt and bring the water to a boil. Reduce the heat and simmer the beets until they are fork-tender, 12 to 15 minutes. Remove them from the heat and drain.

Place the beets and onion in a large bowl. In a separate bowl, whisk together the vinegar, honey, and olive oil with a healthy pinch of salt and pepper. Drizzle half the mixture into the bowl with the beets and onion. Toss to coat and set aside.

Place the torn bread on a baking sheet and drizzle it with olive oil, salt, and pepper. Bake until the bread is golden brown and crisp, 8 to 10 minutes, tossing it once halfway through cooking.

Add the bread to the bowl with the beets and onion. Drizzle in more of the dressing to taste and top with the goat cheese and fresh herbs. If need be, sprinkle with more salt to taste and a drizzle of plain olive oil.

Mushroom Hunter's Stew

SERVES 4

Localize it

Try using red or yellow onions if you can't find leeks. Any wild or cultivated mushroom will work here.

When our buddy Colin and I went mushroom hunting during our month of eating local food, it was cold, dreary, and rainy. I came home chilled to the bone and whipped up this stew with my baskets full of freshly unearthed chanterelles. It is hands down one of the most comforting stews you could ever wish for on a drizzly fall day.

¼ cup cooking fat (page xv)
2 medium leeks, washed, trimmed, and thinly sliced (white and pale green parts only)
2 teaspoons dried thyme
Pinch of crushed red pepper flakes (page 42)
Salt
2 medium-small potatoes, cut into ½-inch chunks

1 pound chanterelle mushrooms, roughly chopped
½ cup dry white wine
1 quart bone broth, veggie stock, or chicken stock (pages 30–31)
1½ cups heavy cream
Freshly ground black pepper

In a large Dutch oven or soup pot over medium heat, add the cooking fat. Once it is warm, add the leeks, thyme, red pepper flakes, and a hefty pinch of salt. Stir often, until softened, about 6 minutes. Add the potatoes and mushrooms and cook, stirring occasionally, until the mushrooms give up some of their liquid and shrink in size, about 8 minutes.

Pour in the wine and cook until some of the liquid evaporates, about 2 minutes. Slowly add the stock, then increase the heat to medium-high and simmer for 20 minutes. Reduce the heat to low, stir in the cream, and cook for 5 more minutes or until just warmed through. Add salt and pepper to taste.

Serve with a side of toasted sourdough bread for dunking.

Honey and Cider Baked Beans

SERVES 8 TO 10
AS A SIDE

Localize it

You can try these with any type of bean, though I'd avoid chickpeas. If you're out of honey, try using maple syrup.

These beans are incredibly easy to make, but like any good baked bean recipe, you have to be patient and give them some time. Let them simmer on the stove all day—the result is well worth the effort.

3 cups dried pinto beans, soaked for at least 8 hours or overnight
½ pound thinly sliced salted pork belly or thick-cut bacon
2 large onions, diced
2 cups dry hard apple cider
¼ cup tomato paste (page 39)
Heaping ½ cup honey
1 tablespoon Dijon mustard
2 teaspoons salt
Freshly ground black pepper

Preheat the oven to 350°F.

Drain the soaked beans and set them aside.

Heat a large Dutch oven over medium-high heat. Add the sliced pork belly or bacon and cook, stirring often, until it is lightly browned (it doesn't need to be completely cooked). Use a slotted spoon to remove the pork from the heat and pour off all but 2 tablespoons of the fat. (Save the extra for another use.)

Add the onions and cook, stirring occasionally, until they start to brown. Add the hard cider and bring it to a low boil. Scrape up any browned bits at the bottom of the pan. Reduce the heat to low and add the tomato paste, honey, mustard, salt, pepper to taste, beans, and reserved pork belly.

Add enough water to the pot to cover the beans.

Cover the pot with a lid and bake for about 5 hours, checking the beans every couple of hours and adding more water as needed to keep them submerged. Cook until the beans are tender and the mixture is thick.

Taste for seasonings and serve hot directly from the pot.

Cornmeal-Crusted Fried Green Tomatoes with Herb Goat Cheese Sauce

SERVES 6

Localize it
Sorry, no swaps here—if you can't find green tomatoes, you can't make fried green tomatoes!

In the Pacific Northwest, tomato season ends almost as quickly as it begins. With cold, short days arriving by mid-September, our tomatoes are slow to ripen and seem to stay green forever—which works perfectly for this delicious dish that makes a lovely appetizer or side and is a great addition to a BLT.

3 green tomatoes, cut into ½-inch slices
Salt
2 large eggs, lightly beaten
2 tablespoons water
1 cup all-purpose flour
1 cup cornmeal
2 teaspoons dried parsley
¼ teaspoon crushed red pepper flakes
½ teaspoon freshly ground black pepper
Neutral high heat oil or ghee for frying
Herb Goat Cheese Dressing (page 36) for serving

Preheat the oven to 250°F.

Sprinkle the sliced tomatoes with a little salt and set them aside on a plate.

In a shallow bowl, whisk together the eggs and 2 tablespoons water; set aside.

Place the flour and cornmeal in two separate bowls. Combine the cornmeal with the parsley, crushed red pepper flakes, a hefty pinch of salt, and the pepper and mix. Set a baking sheet nearby. Dip each tomato slice into the flour, then the egg mixture. Press the tomato into the cornmeal mixture, shaking off the excess. Transfer the tomatoes to the baking sheet. Repeat with the remaining tomato slices, arranging them in a single layer.

In a large heavy-bottom cast-iron skillet over medium heat, pour oil to a depth of ½ inch. Once the oil is hot and beginning to shimmer, use tongs to carefully place the tomato slices in a single layer in the pan (being careful not to drop the tomatoes, as hot oil can splatter up); be mindful not to overcrowd the pan. Fry the tomatoes, in batches, for about 2 minutes on each side or until golden. Drain them on paper towels or a wire rack, then return them to the baking sheet and keep them warm in the oven until ready to serve.

Plate and serve the fried green tomatoes with a drizzle of goat cheese dressing.

Fall Harvest Sheet Pan Salmon and Veggies with Kale Pesto

SERVES 4

Localize it

You could use trout, cod, or even a tuna loin. Keep in mind that cooking times will vary. Swap out the veggies with what you've got on hand. Cauliflower, turnips, and butternut squash would all be great additions. No kale? Substitute another pesto or chimichurri sauce (page 33).

Around these parts, salmon season is all the rage in the fall. Salmon is plentiful and available at most of our local farmers' markets and even at roadside stands, so we stock up and freeze extra for the winter months ahead. This sheet pan supper couldn't be any simpler and is the perfect celebration of autumn in the Pacific Northwest.

FOR THE KALE PESTO
2 to 3 cloves of garlic
3 cups packed kale leaves
    (about 1 small bunch)
¾ cup toasted walnuts
    (or any lightly toasted
    nut or seed)
2 tablespoons red wine vinegar
¾ teaspoon fine-grain sea salt
¼ teaspoon freshly ground
    black pepper
Pinch of crushed red pepper flakes
    (page 42; optional)
½ cup walnut oil or extra-virgin
    olive oil, plus more if desired

FOR THE ROASTING PAN
1 large onion, peeled, cut into
    ½ -inch wedges
3 small beets, halved
    (no need to peel)
2 carrots, chopped into 1-inch pieces
    (no need to peel)
1 small to medium sweet potato,
    cut into 1-inch pieces
    (no need to peel)
8 broccolini stalks
2 tablespoons extra-virgin olive oil
Salt and freshly ground
    black pepper
¼ teaspoon crushed red pepper flakes
4 (5- to 6-ounce) salmon fillets

Preheat the oven to 425°F.

Make the pesto: In a food processor, mince the garlic cloves. Add the kale, walnuts, vinegar, salt, black pepper, and red pepper flakes. With the motor running, drizzle in the oil. Process until the pesto reaches your desired consistency, stopping to scrape down the sides as necessary. Taste and adjust seasonings as needed.

To begin roasting, on a rimmed baking sheet, toss the veggies with olive oil and season them with red pepper flakes and salt and black pepper to taste. Roast them for about 20 minutes, or until they are slightly tender.

Remove the pan from the oven and wedge the salmon fillets between the veggies, skin side down.

Return the pan to the oven and roast for 10 to 15 minutes more, until the salmon reaches desired doneness and the veggies are tender.

Serve salmon and veggies family-style, with kale pesto for drizzling.

Hearty Chicken and Vegetable Soup

SERVES 8

There's a reason why chicken soup is said to be "good for the soul"—I believe something truly magical happens when you simmer a nourishing broth with loads of vegetables, herbs, and juicy chicken. The flavor of this rustic soup is rich and comforting, and when served with a hunk of bread and a cup of tea, it simply cannot be beat.

Carcass and bones from one
  4- to 5-pound roasted chicken,
  with some of the meat still on
  (page 211)
4 cups chicken stock (page 31)
2 medium onions, peeled,
  thinly sliced
2 celery stalks, cut into
  ¼-inch-thick slices
2 medium carrots, sliced into
  ¼-inch-thick rounds

1 medium parsnip, sliced into
  ¼-inch-thick rounds
3 medium potatoes, cut into
  ½-inch pieces
3 thyme sprigs
1 bay leaf
Salt and freshly ground
  black pepper
Crushed red pepper flakes
  (page 42)

In a large pot, place the bones and carcass. Cover with the broth and 4 cups water. Bring the liquid to a boil over medium-high heat, reduce it to a simmer, and cook for 20 minutes. Skim any foam or fat from the broth as necessary.

Remove the bones and carcass with tongs or a slotted spoon; set them aside to cool. Add the onions, celery, carrots, parsnip, potatoes, thyme sprigs, and bay leaf to the broth, bring it back to a simmer, and cook until the vegetables are tender, about 25 minutes.

Meanwhile, when the carcass and bones are cool enough to handle, pick off the meat and shred it into bite-sized pieces. Add the meat to the stock and remove the bay leaf and thyme sprigs. Season to taste with plenty of salt and black pepper and a dash of red pepper flakes.

Ladle the soup into bowls and serve it with toasted sourdough bread (page 31).

Kohlrabi Hash Browns

SERVES 4

Localize it

Try potatoes or rutabagas instead of kohlrabies—or use a mixture of all!

We grow a lot of kohlrabi at Tumbleweed, for two reasons: It flourishes in our climate, and I absolutely adore this crazy-looking vegetable. It's crunchy and mildly sweet, and can be added to pretty much any salad, slaw, or soup. This is a fun way to prepare kohlrabi if you're out of potatoes or just looking for something a little different to jazz up your morning breakfast routine.

1 pound kohlrabies
  (2 small to medium), peeled
Salt and freshly ground
  black pepper

1 teaspoon dried thyme
Pinch of crushed red pepper flakes
  (page 42)
¼ cup cooking fat (page xv)

On a large-holed cheese grater or with the grating attachment on a food processor, grate the kohlrabies.

Place the grated kohlrabi on a clean dish towel. Twist the towel to remove as much moisture as possible (you might need to do this in two batches).

Transfer the grated kohlrabi to a medium-sized bowl and toss it with the salt, black pepper, thyme, and red pepper flakes.

In a large, well-seasoned cast-iron pan over medium heat, warm the cooking fat. Spread the kohlrabi mixture in an even layer and press it down with a spatula. Let it cook, undisturbed, for about 2 minutes.

Stir the mixture, press it down again, and cook for another 2 minutes. Repeat in 2-minute intervals, flipping the hash browns in sections once they are solid enough to do so, until the kohlrabi shreds are golden brown and crispy, 5 to 8 more minutes.

Transfer the hash browns to a lined plate and let them drain for a minute.

Season with additional salt and pepper to taste and serve hot.

Farmhouse Chicken Pot Pie

SERVES 6

Localize it

Try this with any variety of vegetables: rutabagas, kohlrabies, potatoes, sweet potatoes, winter squash, or even beets.

At our house, it isn't a proper Sunday evening in October without a chicken pot pie baking in the oven. This recipe not only packs a bunch of seasonal vegetables into one flaky pie crust, but it's also cozy, delicious, and perfect for a chilly night. My mom used to use Martha Stewart's recipe, and she passed it down to me—so this is my farm-fresh twist on a classic!

FOR THE CRUST
(see Pumpkin Pot Pie with
   Sausage and Kale, page 62)

FOR THE FILLING AND ASSEMBLY
5 tablespoons cooking fat
   (page xv)
1 medium yellow onion,
   finely chopped
2 teaspoons dried thyme
2 teaspoons dried rosemary
Salt and freshly ground black pepper
Pinch of crushed red pepper flakes
   (page 42)

4 medium carrots, finely chopped
2 parsnips, finely chopped
4 cloves of garlic, minced
½ cup all-purpose flour
4 cups chicken bone broth
   or stock (pages 30–31)
1 cup frozen peas
3 cups shredded cooked chicken
   (page 211)
¼ cup chopped fresh parsley
1 egg
2 tablespoons cream or milk

Preheat the oven to 375°F.

Make the crust: Cube the cold butter into ½-inch dice with a sharp knife and place it in the freezer to cool back down after handling (don't skip this part). In a food processor, pulse together the flour and salt. Add the cubed butter and pulse 12 to 16 times, or until the mixture resembles coarse meal, with a few pea-sized pieces of butter remaining. With the machine running, slowly pour in 3 tablespoons of the water. Pulse until the dough begins to form a ball (it may still be crumbly, and that's okay as long as when you pinch it, the mixture holds together). If it seems too dry, add a touch more ice water. Do not overmix.

Form the dough into a disk, wrap it tightly in plastic, and refrigerate until firm, 1 hour or overnight (or freeze it for up to a month).

Make the filling: In a large, deep cast-iron pot over medium-high heat, add the cooking fat and swirl to coat the pan. Add the onion, thyme, rosemary, salt, black pepper, and red pepper flakes. Cook, stirring occasionally, until the onions begin to soften and become fragrant, about 5 minutes. Add the carrots and parsnips and cook until softened, about 8 minutes. Add the garlic and cook until fragrant, about 30 seconds. Add the flour and stir to coat the vegetables.

Slowly add the broth, whisking constantly until the sauce is smooth (a few small clumps are okay). Bring the mixture to a boil, immediately reduce the heat, and simmer until thickened, 5 to 7 minutes. Stir in the peas, chicken, and parsley. Remove the pot from the heat and let the filling cool a bit. If you aren't using a cast-iron pan, you can then transfer the filling into a 2-quart baking dish.

In a small bowl, make the egg wash by whisking together the egg and cream or milk.

On a floured work surface, roll out the dough into a ⅛-inch-thick round. Place it over the pot or baking dish (being careful not to burn yourself if you're using the cast-iron pot) and fold the overhang inward while pinching to crimp the edge. Cut vents in the dough. Brush the crust with the egg wash. Place the dish on a rimmed baking sheet (this will protect your oven floor from any bubbling mixture spilling out!) and bake until the crust is golden brown and the filling is bubbling around the edges, 45 to 50 minutes.

Transfer the pot pie to a wire rack and let it cool for 15 minutes before serving.

Open-Faced Sloppy Joes

SERVES 4

Localize it

Any ground meat will work (turkey, chicken, lamb).

When we were kids, we loved sloppy joes because it was the one time that being messy was totally acceptable (and encouraged!). The messier your sloppy joe was, the better it tasted. My take on this tradition is no-fuss and delicious. It is a little lighter than my childhood favorite and incorporates local mushrooms and fresh thyme for more flavor—plus, it can be eaten with a fork and knife! Pair it with a fresh salad for a complete meal.

1 tablespoon cooking fat (page xv)
1 small onion, finely chopped
1 tablespoon minced thyme
½ teaspoon crushed red pepper flakes (page 42)
1 pound ground beef
2 cups chopped mushrooms (any variety or mix)

3 cloves of garlic, minced
½ cup tomato paste (page 39)
2 tablespoons red wine vinegar
1 tablespoon honey
¼ teaspoon salt
¾ teaspoon freshly ground black pepper
4 slices sourdough bread (page 44), toasted

Heat a large, well-seasoned cast-iron pan over medium-high. Add your cooking fat and swirl to coat the pan. Add the onion, thyme, and crushed red pepper flakes and cook, stirring occasionally, until the onion is soft and fragrant, about 5 minutes. Add the beef and cook for about 4 minutes or until it is browned and no longer pink, using a wooden spoon to crumble the meat up a bit.

Add the mushrooms and garlic; cook for 3 minutes or until the garlic is tender. Add the tomato paste, vinegar, honey, salt, and black pepper; cook for 5 minutes or until the mushrooms are tender, have shrunk in size, and their liquid has evaporated.

Spoon about ½ cup of the beef mixture onto each slice of toasted bread and serve.

Honey Braised Turnips and Greens with Bacon

SERVES 4
AS A SIDE

Localize it

Try radishes instead of turnips for a fun twist. If your turnip greens are pretty gnarly-looking or old, swap them out for Swiss chard, spinach, or beet greens.

Turnips and bacon are a match made in heaven. This simple side dish is a great addition to any dinner party or potluck, and would make a terrific accompaniment to a holiday meal. Bonus: It tastes great warm or at room temperature, so it's easy to prepare in advance!

4 slices thick-cut bacon, roughly chopped
2 pounds baby turnips with greens, turnips sliced in half, greens roughly chopped
¾ cup chicken bone broth or stock (pages 30–31)

2 tablespoons honey
2 tablespoons apple cider vinegar
1 tablespoon Dijon mustard
Salt and freshly ground black pepper
2 tablespoons unsalted butter

In a large cast-iron skillet over medium heat, cook the chopped bacon, stirring it frequently, until it is browned and lightly crisp, 5 to 7 minutes. Transfer it to a paper-towel-lined plate to drain.

Drain all but 1 tablespoon of the bacon grease into a mason jar and reserve it for another use. Add the halved turnips, broth, honey, vinegar, and mustard to the skillet; season with salt and pepper to taste. Bring the mixture to a simmer. Cover the pan, reduce the heat to medium-low, and cook until the turnips are tender, 8 to 10 minutes.

Uncover the pan and increase the heat to medium. Stir in the turnip greens and add the butter. Cook, stirring occasionally, until the sauce thickens to a glaze that evenly coats the turnips, about 10 minutes.

Top with the bacon and serve.

Apple Pie

SERVES 8

Localize it

Swap out the apples for pears or even use chopped-up roasted winter squash or pumpkin for a fun twist on pumpkin pie. You can drizzle a little more honey on the finished pie for added sweetness if you like.

My girlfriend Chesua makes the best damn apple pie around! She also makes the best pizza crust (you may remember from my first cookbook). This is her pie recipe. She uses local apples from our neighboring farm and honey from down the road as the sweetener. It's easy to prepare, and the crust is the absolute best, flakiest pie crust around. Serve it warm with a nice big scoop of ice cream from a local dairy.

FOR THE CRUST
1 cup (2 sticks) cold butter
2½ cups all-purpose flour
½ teaspoon salt
⅓ to ⅔ cup ice water

FOR THE FILLING AND ASSEMBLY
5 large Granny Smith or other baking apples, peeled, cored, and sliced (about 6 cups)
½ cup plus 2 tablespoons honey, warmed on the stovetop until pourable

2 teaspoons ground cinnamon
Pinch of ground cloves
Pinch of freshly grated nutmeg
Pinch of sea salt
⅓ cup all-purpose flour, plus more for sprinkling
1 egg
1 tablespoon cream or milk
Pinch of flaky sea salt (optional)

Make the crust: Cube the cold butter into ½-inch dice with a sharp knife and place it in the freezer to cool back down after handling (don't skip this part!). In a food processor, pulse together the flour and salt. Add the cubed butter and pulse 10 to 14 times or until the mixture resembles coarse meal, with a few pea-sized pieces of butter remaining. With the machine running, slowly pour in ⅓ cup of the water. Pulse until the dough begins to form a ball (it may still be crumbly, and that's okay as long as when you pinch it the mixture holds together). If it seems too dry, add more of the ice water. Do not overmix.

Divide the dough in half. Shape each into a round, flat disk and wrap it in plastic. Refrigerate the rounds for 1 hour or overnight (or freeze them for up to one month).

Preheat the oven to 400°F.

Make the filling: In a large bowl, mix the apple slices, ½ cup of the warm honey, the cinnamon, cloves, nutmeg, sea salt, and flour.

In a small bowl, make an egg wash by whisking together the egg and milk or cream. Set it aside.

Roll out one of the dough rounds and use it to line the bottom of a 9-inch pie pan so that it hangs a bit over the edges. Sprinkle the bottom of the crust with a little flour (this helps keep the crust from getting soggy). Carefully pour the apple mixture into the prepared pie crust, filling in gaps and holes along the way. Your pie filling will seem like way too much, creating a mountain of apples in the middle. Don't worry, it cooks down.

Roll out the remaining dough round to form the top crust. To transfer the crust to the pie, place a rolling pin over one side of the crust. Very carefully (and loosely) roll the crust around the pin and bring it to the pie. Unroll the crust and drape it over the pie filling. Don't worry if tears appear—you can patch them up. Use kitchen scissors to trim the edge of the crust to about 1 inch over the rim. Tuck the edge of the top crust under the edge of the bottom crust and crimp the two together with your fingers. Brush the entire top crust with the egg wash and cut four or five slits for ventilation.

Place the pie on a sheet pan and bake it for 15 minutes. Then reduce the temperature to 350°F and bake for an additional 40 to 50 minutes or until the crust is golden brown. If the edges start to brown too fast, cover them in aluminum foil.

Remove the pie from the oven and drizzle it with the remaining 2 tablespoons honey and a sprinkle of flaky sea salt if desired for a sweet-salty crust!

Let the pie cool for 15 minutes before slicing and serving.

Pumpkin and Sage Frittata

SERVES 6

Localize it

Localize it

Use any variety of winter squash—butternut, acorn, delicata—or even a sweet potato. If you do use the pie pumpkin, there's no need to peel it, as the skin is edible and will become tender when cooked.

The beauty of a frittata is that you can use any mix of seasonal vegetables and any type of eggs—chicken, duck, or goose—that you've got on hand. There are no rules. I love this fall frittata because it celebrates some of my favorite ingredients. The pumpkin, sage, and nutmeg bring warming flavors to every bite, and the goat cheese becomes melt-in-your-mouth delicious. Leftovers are equally good and can be eaten warm, room temperature, or even chilled.

8 tablespoons cooking fat (page xv)
1 (2-pound) pie pumpkin, halved, seeded, and cut into ¼-inch cubes no need to peel (about 4 cups)
Salt and freshly ground black pepper
Hefty pinch of freshly grated nutmeg
1 small yellow onion, halved and very thinly sliced

1 tablespoon minced sage, plus 4 or 5 whole sage leaves for topping
10 large eggs
3 tablespoons heavy cream
8 ounces goat cheese, crumbled

Place an oven rack 5 inches below the heat and preheat the broiler.

Warm 2 tablespoons of the cooking fat in a 10-inch cast-iron pan over medium-high heat. Add half of the squash, season it with salt, pepper, and nutmeg, and cook, stirring occasionally, until it softens and begins to brown, about 7 minutes. Transfer it to a bowl and repeat with the remaining squash, again using 2 tablespoons of the cooking fat.

Warm another tablespoon of the cooking fat in the pan. Add the onion, season it with salt and pepper, and cook, stirring occasionally, until it is tender and beginning to brown, about 7 minutes. Transfer it to the bowl with the squash.

Reduce the heat to medium and melt 2 tablespoons of the fat. Add the minced sage and cook until it is bright green and lightly crisp, about 2 minutes. Remove it from the pan and set it aside. Then add the whole sage leaves to the pan and repeat the same process to crisp them. Set them aside and wipe out the pan.

In a large bowl, whisk together the eggs and cream. Stir in the cheese, pumpkin, onion, and minced sage.

Place the remaining 1 tablespoon of fat in the pan over medium heat. When it is warm, add the egg mixture and cook, using a rubber spatula to lift the cooked edges and allow the uncooked eggs to flow underneath, 3 to 4 minutes. Top the frittata with the whole sage leaves and continue to cook 3 to 5 minutes longer or until the eggs are set.

Place the pan in the oven and broil the frittata until it sets and puffs up slightly, 2 to 3 minutes. (Watch the frittata carefully to ensure it doesn't burn.)

Cut into wedges and serve.

Dad's French Onion Soup

SERVES 4

Localize it

Any type of onion or shallot will work well here. Fresh out of white wine? Try red. Swap out the dried thyme for parsley or rosemary for a different twist.

This is my dad's famous onion soup—at least, it's pretty famous within my family! It's one of his most-requested dishes, and we can never get enough of it. Instead of melting a cheese like Gruyère over the bowl, we top our soup with a cheddar cheese toast that's perfect for dipping. Serve it with a nice glass of red wine for the perfect cold-weather meal.

¼ cup butter or cooking fat of choice (page xv)
3 large red onions, peeled and thinly sliced
3 large yellow onions, peeled and thinly sliced
2 bay leaves
1 teaspoon dried thyme, or more to taste
Salt
2 cloves of garlic, minced

½ cup dry white wine
8 cups beef stock or bone broth (pages 30–31)
2 bay leaves
Freshly ground black pepper
8 slices sourdough bread (page 44), cut 1 inch thick
Olive oil
1½ cups grated sharp cheddar or another hard, slightly salty cheese

In a 5- to 6-quart heavy-bottom pot over medium, heat 3 tablespoons of the cooking fat. Add the onions, bay leaves, thyme, and a hefty pinch of salt. Toss to coat and cook, stirring often, until the onions have softened, 15 to 20 minutes.

Increase the heat to medium high and add the remaining tablespoon of cooking fat. Continue cooking, stirring often, until the onions are very fragrant and have cooked down a bit, about 15 minutes.

Add the garlic and cook for 1 more minute. Add the white wine and deglaze the pot, using a wooden spoon to break up some of the brown bits from the bottom.

Add the stock. Bring the soup to a simmer, cover the pot, and lower the heat to maintain a low simmer. Cook for 45 minutes to 1 hour.

Season the soup with more salt and black pepper to taste. Discard the bay leaves.

Meanwhile, place a rack in the upper third of the oven and preheat it to 450°F. Brush both sides of the bread with olive oil and place them in the oven on a baking sheet. Toast until they are lightly browned on top, 5 to 7 minutes.

Remove the toasts from the oven, turn them over, and top each with grated cheese. Bake until the cheese is bubbly and lightly browned.

Ladle the soup into a bowls, place one cheesy toast on top of each, and serve immediately.

Honey and Thyme Roasted Carrots

SERVES 4
AS A SIDE

Localize it

You could roast parsnips or even beets. Try swapping the honey for maple syrup and sage for the thyme for a different herby flavor.

Side dishes don't get easier than these carrots. I have served these many times when we have company over at the farm, and while they go well with just about anything, I particularly love serving them when we're roasting chicken thighs. There's just something about sweet, earthy carrots and juicy chicken that's hard to beat.

1 large bunch carrots, preferably multicolored
2 tablespoons melted butter
1 tablespoon honey, melted until pourable

Pinch each of salt and freshly ground black pepper
3 or 4 sprigs fresh thyme

Preheat the oven to 425°F.

In a large bowl, toss the carrots with the butter, honey, salt, pepper, and thyme until well coated. Arrange them in an single layer on a baking sheet and roast until they are browned and caramelized, about 30 minutes. Toss the carrots halfway through cooking.

Serve warm or at room temperature.

Tre-Fin Tuna Chowder

SERVES 4

Localize it

Use any white-fleshed fish that you have access to. Just keep in mind that cooking times and flavors will vary slightly.

After my life-changing experience on the albacore tuna boat, I came home with a TON of fresh tuna during our first rainstorm of the season. I whipped up this chowder to warm us up while I shared stories of my epic fishing adventure. It is creamy and indulgent and hearty and everything you want in a fish chowder. Tip: Don't skimp on the chimichurri—it cuts through the richness and adds some zing!

4 slices of thick-cut bacon, chopped
2 tablespoons unsalted butter
2 medium yellow onions, chopped (about 2 cups)
Salt and freshly ground black pepper
½ cup dry white wine
2 large potatoes (about 1 pound), cut into ½-inch pieces

3 cups chicken stock, plus more if needed (page 31)
1 tablespoon thyme leaves
1½ pounds tuna loin, cut into 2-inch pieces
1½ cups heavy cream
¼ to ½ cup chimichurri sauce (page 33)

In a large Dutch oven or other heavy pot over medium heat, cook the bacon, stirring it often, until it is browned but not crisp, 8 to 10 minutes. Transfer it with a slotted spoon to paper towels.

Add the butter and onions to the drippings in the pot; season with salt and pepper. Cook, stirring occasionally, until the onions are soft, 5 to 8 minutes.

Stir in the wine, bring to a boil, scraping up any brown bits on the bottom of the pot, and cook until the wine is reduced by half. Add the potatoes and enough stock to cover them. Add the thyme and bring the mixture to a boil. Reduce the heat and simmer until the potatoes are tender, 10 to 15 minutes.

Season the tuna with salt and pepper and place it on top of the potatoes. Cover the pot and cook (the liquid should be barely simmering) until the fish is opaque throughout, 5 to 7 minutes (thicker pieces will take longer to cook). Stir in the cream and the reserved bacon and return the chowder to a simmer. Season with salt and pepper.

Divide the soup into bowls and stir in 1 to 2 tablespoons of chimichurri just before serving.

Green Bean Casserole with Walnut Bacon Crumble

SERVES 6
AS A SIDE

Localize it

Any type of nut or seed will work for the topping. I've made this recipe with Brussels sprouts in place of the green beans, and it's a fabulous substitute. Swap out the chanterelle mushrooms for any local wild or cultivated mushroom.

I love the spirit behind this traditional holiday dish, and I have to say that my version is quite possibly the best I've ever tasted. I use wild foraged chanterelle mushrooms in the filling, and the crumble topping has the most unique, crunchy, sweet, salty, nutty flavor. If you're afraid that local green beans won't be readily available at Thanksgiving, make sure to stock up on them earlier in the fall and freeze them!

FOR THE TOPPING
4 slices thick-cut bacon, finely chopped
1 medium onion, diced
½ cup walnuts
½ cup finely chopped parsley

FOR THE BEANS AND SAUCE
1 pound fresh green beans, rinsed and trimmed

2 tablespoons unsalted butter
12 ounces chanterelle mushrooms, roughly chopped
Hefty pinch of salt and freshly ground black pepper
2 cloves of garlic, minced
¼ teaspoon freshly grated nutmeg
2 tablespoons all-purpose flour
1 cup chicken broth (page 30)
1 cup heavy cream

Preheat the oven to 475°F.

Make the topping: In a large cast-iron skillet over medium heat, cook the bacon until it is lightly crisp (it will cook a little more in the oven, so no need to get it extra crispy). With a slotted spoon, transfer the bacon to a paper-towel-lined plate to drain. Add the onion to the bacon drippings (there should be about 1 tablespoon in the skillet; if there's way more than that, pour out some and save it for future use). Cook the onion until it is soft and tender, about 8 minutes. Transfer it to a bowl.

Add the walnuts to the same pan and cook, shaking the pan often, until they are lightly golden, about 5 minutes. Add the walnuts to the bowl with the onion and crumble in the bacon. Add the parsley and toss the whole mixture well. Set aside.

Wipe out the skillet (you'll be using it again).

Make the beans: Bring a large pot of heavily salted water to a boil. Add the beans and blanch them for 5 minutes. While they cook, prepare a large bowl of ice water. Drain the beans in a colander and immediately plunge them into the ice water to stop the cooking. Drain them again and set them aside.

Make the sauce: Melt the butter in the cast-iron skillet set over medium-high heat. Add the mushrooms and a hefty pinch of salt and pepper and cook, stirring occasionally, until the mushrooms begin to give up some of their liquid, 4 to 5 minutes. Add the garlic and nutmeg and continue to cook for another 1 to 2 minutes. Sprinkle the flour over the mixture and stir to combine. Cook for 1 minute. Add the broth and simmer for 1 minute. Decrease the heat to medium-low and add the cream. Cook until the mixture thickens, stirring occasionally, 6 to 8 minutes.

Remove the pan from the heat and add the green beans. Sprinkle them evenly with the bacon and onion mixture and bake until bubbly, approximately 15 minutes.

Serve immediately.

Pork and Collard Greens

SERVES 6
AS A SIDE

Localize it

Try using any part of the hog: thick bacon, leftover ham steaks, or leftover pork butt. Swap in kale or Swiss chard for the collards.

Pork and collard greens are a Southern classic that I happily started preparing up north once we got into farming. I love the hearty texture of collards, which stand up well to cooking, and here their slightly bitter bite is complemented by salty smoked ham and sweet caramelized onions. I make this dish pretty often in the fall—once you try it, you will, too!

1 pound meaty smoked ham hocks
2 medium yellow onions, sliced into 2-inch wedges
4 large cloves of garlic, minced
½ teaspoon crushed red pepper flakes (page 42)
2 quarts bone broth, veggie stock, or water (pages 30–31)

2 bunches collard greens (about 3 pounds), woody stems trimmed and leaves cut into thick ribbons
Salt and freshly ground black pepper
Red wine vinegar

In a large, deep cast-iron pot or Dutch oven, combine the ham hocks, onions, garlic, red pepper flakes, and broth and bring the mixture to a boil. Reduce the heat to low, cover, and cook at a bare simmer until the hocks are very tender, 2 to 3 hours.

Transfer the ham hocks to a cutting board, and when they're cool enough to handle, pull the meat from the bones. Discard the bones (or save them for stock). Chop the meat into chunks and return it to the pot.

Add the collard greens, using a wooden spoon to press them down to submerge them in the liquid. Return to a simmer and cook, uncovered, until the collards are very tender, about 30 minutes. Season with salt and pepper. Add a splash of red wine vinegar to taste, then serve.

Polish Sausages with Apples and Sauerkraut

SERVES 4

Localize it

Use any type of sausage you have and try swapping the apples for pears if that's what you can find. Note—a lot of farmers' [apostrophe] markets have local vendors who make their own jarred sauerkraut.

Well, damn, this turned out to be one of my favorite recipes in the whole book. I had no idea I could love sausage and sauerkraut so much! We first made this dish when our neighbors came over for dinner, and it's since become one of my go-tos—especially for that same couple, who still request it often. It's great for entertaining because it comes together so easily, and it's super flavorful and filling.

½ pound bacon, cut into
    1-inch pieces
1½ pounds Polish sausages
    (kielbasa or bratwurst)
1 large onion, peeled, diced
Cooking fat, if needed (page xv)

1 (2-pound) jar of sauerkraut
    (about 32 ounces) with juice
3 tablespoons honey
2 apples, cored, diced
Minced parsley for serving

In a large heavy-bottom frying pan over medium-high heat, cook the bacon. With a slotted spoon, remove the bacon and set it aside to drain on paper towels.

Add the sausages to the bacon fat in the pan and cook until they are browned all over, about 10 minutes. Remove the sausages from the pan and set them aside. Add the onion to the same skillet and sauté until it is soft and translucent (if the pan gets a bit dry, add a bit of cooking fat). Add the sauerkraut, honey, and apples to the skillet, stir, and simmer over low heat for 1 hour. Stir occasionally and add a bit of water if necessary to prevent burning.

Add the sausages to the sauerkraut, along with the reserved bacon. Simmer the mixture together for another 10 to 15 minutes.

Top with minced parsley and serve warm.

Roasted Cauliflower with Bread Crumbs

SERVES 4
AS A SIDE

Localize it

Use finely chopped hazelnuts, walnuts, or almonds in place of bread crumbs.

Roasted cauliflower is one of those humble side dishes that doesn't seem very exciting—yet folks always come back for seconds, and there are never any leftovers. The roasting process turns otherwise bland cauliflower slightly sweet and nutty, and if you cut your florets on the smaller side, they can get a slight char and crunch to them. Topped with homemade bread crumbs and sharp cheese, this "humble" side may end up stealing the show!

1 head of cauliflower, broken into florets
¼ cup melted cooking fat (page xv)
¼ teaspoon crushed red pepper flakes (page 42)
1 teaspoon dried thyme
½ cup homemade bread crumbs (page 47)
½ cup freshly grated sharp cheese
Salt and freshly ground black pepper
¼ cup minced parsley

Preheat the oven to 425°F.

Toss the cauliflower with the cooking fat, red pepper flakes, dried thyme, bread crumbs, cheese, salt, and pepper.

Spread the florets out on the baking sheet and roast until they are golden brown and tender, 30 to 40 minutes.

Remove the cauliflower from the oven and immediately sprinkle on the minced parsley. Give it a good toss and serve warm.

Broccoli Cheddar Soup

SERVES 4

Oh, man, this childhood favorite just got a MAJOR upgrade! It's not quite as heavy as the one I grew up eating, but it still brings me back to my parents' kitchen, where I would dip hunks of bread into a big old bowl of this soup! It tastes even better the next day heated up and, preferably, served with a grilled cheese sandwich (page 118)!

6 tablespoons unsalted butter
1 large yellow onion, finely chopped
¼ teaspoon freshly grated nutmeg
2 cloves of garlic, finely chopped
Salt and freshly ground black pepper
¼ cup white wine
2 pounds broccoli florets
    with stems, chopped

3 cups chicken or vegetable broth
    (page 30)
¼ cup all-purpose flour
2 cups whole milk
¼ cup chopped parsley
8 ounces very sharp cheddar,
    grated, plus more for topping

In a large, deep cast-iron pot or soup pan, melt 3 tablespoons of the butter over medium heat. Add the onion and nutmeg and cook, stirring occasionally, until the butter foams up a bit and the nutmeg is fragrant, about 3 minutes. Add the garlic and season generously with salt and pepper. Cook, stirring occasionally, until the veggies are softened and translucent, 5 to 8 minutes.

Add the wine and bring to a simmer. Cook, stirring up any browned bits, until it's reduced by half. Add the broccoli and ½ cup of the broth and cook, stirring occasionally, until the broccoli is bright green and slightly tender, 8 to 10 minutes. Transfer it to a medium bowl and set aside.

Heat the remaining 3 tablespoons butter in the same pot over medium heat (don't worry about any remaining vegetable bits). Add the flour and whisk constantly for 2 to 3 minutes or until it has browned up a bit and thickened.

Gradually whisk in the remaining chicken broth and stir until most of the clumps dissolve. Pour in the milk and add the parsley. Bring the mixture to a simmer. Stir in the cheese and all but 1 cup of the reserved broccoli mixture.

Reduce the heat to low and simmer until the liquid has thickened and the broccoli is tender, 25 to 30 minutes.

Using a hand blender or after transferring the soup to a regular blender, puree it to the desired consistency. Sometimes I like this completely smooth, and other times I like a little texture to it!

Season the soup with salt and pepper and ladle it into bowls. Top it with the remaining chopped broccoli for a little added crunch and a sprinkling of cheddar.

Apple, Kohlrabi, and Hazelnut Slaw

SERVES 4
AS A SIDE

Localize it

Use a pear instead of an apple. Try olive oil or another nut oil in place of hazelnut oil. If you can't find kohlrabi, skip it or add thinly sliced broccoli stems. Swap the hazelnuts for walnuts, pecans, or almonds.

This autumnal slaw is our new favorite Thanksgiving side. It's a breeze to prepare and is fresh, flavorful, and the perfect complement to all the heavier sides on the table. It's also great served alongside pork tenderloin or my Simple Roasted Pork Shoulder (page 122) for an easy weeknight dinner.

1 large apple, cored and cut into matchsticks
1 medium kohlrabi, peeled and cut into matchsticks
¼ cup finely chopped red onion
¼ cup toasted chopped hazelnuts
¼ cup hazelnut oil
1 tablespoon apple cider vinegar
2 teaspoons honey
1 teaspoon whole grain mustard
Pinch of crushed red pepper flakes (page 42)
¼ cup finely chopped parsley, plus additional for serving
Hefty pinch of salt

In a large bowl, mix all the ingredients and toss to combine.

Garnish with additional parsley, if desired, and serve.

Winter

There's no need to set an alarm clock in the winter. The sound of the snowplow at the end of our driveway jolts us awake throughout the snowy season. And while it's not my favorite noise, it does get us out of bed quicker than any alarm clock. When we hear the snowplow, we know there's a full day ahead of shoveling, raking, and removing snow from our greenhouses and other farm structures. Folks always assume that farmers (at least in our area) take the winters off. But the truth is, in the heart of winter, we must be vigilant to ensure the farm, fences, and buildings stay intact. Winter storms pose a major threat to our livelihood, and if we don't stay on top of it, the snow can destroy our beloved farm.

It's on these dark and bitter-cold early winter mornings when I question where we have chosen to plant our roots and spend our days. But after the first cup of strong, hot coffee (made from beans that our friends roast right up the road from our farm) and a quick rummage through the fridge to locate bacon, eggs, and cream, I quickly change my frame of mind. Taylor usually heads out to chop a little wood to stoke the fire that is barely burning after the long night, and I get to work making us a hearty breakfast. Fried bacon from our fall pig harvest, along with eggs quickly scrambled with onions, frozen peppers from our stockpile in the freezer, dried herbs, and a hefty glug of cream from our neighbor's cows. I'll warm up the biscuits that I make weekly and give them a healthy smear of butter, and voilà! After about fifteen minutes, I'll plop a pile of food on the table, and Taylor and I will quietly savor each bite.

And while the wintertime at the farm is basically a full-time job of keeping things from falling apart, it's also the time to cozy up in the kitchen with slow stews on the stovetop and to break out those summer goodies from the freezer. Cracking open a jar of pesto or tomato sauce and blanching some cherished frozen greens create bright spots in otherwise heavy meals. But the reality is winter is when our bodies are craving heartier food. Meat, grains, and root vegetables taste better in the winter than at any other time of the year; these meals feel like pure nourishment.

It's easy to feel trapped and isolated in the dead of winter. There are some days when we don't see another human or even leave the property. But there are definitely occasions during the darkest of months that light me up and give me so much gratitude for this season. Sometimes when we're snowed in at the farm in midwinter, we like to throw impromptu "chest freezer" dinner parties. Our neighbors snowshoe over, and we usually defrost a large roast, gather some root veggies from the barn, whip up some buttermilk biscuits, and crack open a few bottles of local wine. It's occasions like these that remind me of how, no matter what, we can still eat amazing food, be surrounded by so much love and laughter, and never leave the comfort of home. Even on the darkest of days, we can rise up and celebrate what we're so lucky to have. Nourishment, a cozy home, and great friends to share it all with.

The challenges of eating locally in winter are very real in the Pacific Northwest. I realize not everyone lives and works on a small vegetable farm, but it's relatively easy to get your hands on winter veggies in many communities. Wintertime CSAs and farmers' markets are growing in popularity, and many small grocery stores source local root vegetables during the winter. Lots of farmers are installing high tunnels for season extension to grow fresh leafy greens during the winter, too. And if you can find the time to stock up on tomatoes at your farmers' market in August and September and put some away in the freezer, you'll thank yourself a million times over when you open a jar in the middle of February. If all you have to do is put on your slippers and go out to your chest freezer to grab some meat, bone broth, and canned tomatoes, you can still enjoy amazing food even if the plow isn't working.

My cooking style in winter is focused on roasts, soups, stews, and cozy meals that maybe take a little more time to prepare than the kinds of dishes I make the rest of the year, but that's the beauty of winter. In the midst of all the damp, cold weather, it's comforting to know that you can find so much warmth in your kitchen. Getting people together becomes even

Even on the darkest of days, we can rise up and celebrate what we're so lucky to have.

more important because it's during these oftentimes lonely days of winter that people need each other more than ever. Getting through it together and sharing good food is sort of what this time of year is all about for us. We crave connection and community to combat the isolation of the weather, the darkness of the days.

By mid-February, I used to find myself wishing winter away because it does seem to go on for so long. Just like everyone else, I start to crave light, warmth, and freshness. But lately I've been trying hard to really just simmer in the harshness of it. The cold and the dark are beautiful in their own way. And when you don't think you can stomach another pot roast, remember that this is the nourishment that is available right now, and it is temporary. Eventually, the ground will thaw. The snow will melt. There will be greens and tomatoes and corn and peaches. Try to practice patience and bathe in that cold moonlight, because everything will be just fine.

Cozy Lentil Stew with Kale and Parsnips

SERVES 4 TO 6

Localize it

Swap out the carrots and parsnips for a sweet potato and turnip. Instead of kale, try tossing in some spinach or chopped collard greens.

There's something so comforting about a bowl of warm lentil stew. It's a staple from my childhood, super nutritious, and will keep you and yours warm for hours! This version is one of my favorites because it includes two of my most loved winter staples—parsnips and kale. The parsnips lend a sweet, earthy flavor, while the kale becomes tender and adds a mellow bite.

3 tablespoons cooking fat (page xv)
1 large yellow or red onion, finely chopped
1½ teaspoons smoked paprika
1 teaspoon ground cumin
¼ teaspoon crushed red pepper flakes (page 42)
Salt and freshly ground black pepper
1 cup chopped carrots
½ cup chopped parsnips

3 cloves of garlic, finely chopped
3 tablespoons tomato paste (page 39)
¼ cup dry red wine
1½ cups brown lentils
4 cups vegetable broth (page 30)
1 bunch of kale, finely chopped (about 5 cups)
1 bay leaf
Plain full-fat yogurt for serving

In a Dutch oven over medium heat, melt the cooking fat. Add the onion, paprika, cumin, red pepper flakes, and a hefty pinch each of salt and pepper. Cook, stirring to coat the onion in the spice mixture until fragrant, about 1 minute. Add the carrots and parsnips and cook, stirring occasionally, until the vegetables begin to soften, about 5 minutes. Add the garlic and tomato paste. Cook for about 1 minute longer. Pour in the wine and bring the mixture to a boil. Use a wooden spoon or spatula to scrape up any brown bits. Reduce the heat and cook until most of the liquid has evaporated.

Add the lentils. Cook, stirring often, until the lentils are coated in the spices and veggies. Add the broth and 2 cups water and toss in the kale and bay leaf. Bring to a boil. Then reduce the heat and simmer until the lentils are tender, about 30 minutes.

Ladle the soup into bowls and stir a dollop of yogurt into each. Serve with crusty bread and a pinch more of salt and pepper to taste.

Biscuits and Gravy

Localize it

Swap out the pork for turkey, chicken, or duck sausage.

When I told Taylor I wanted to re-create American classics in this book, he told me with a straight face, "You need to include a biscuits and gravy recipe." This is his go-to diner order and one of his very favorite meals. With his help and enthusiastic taste-testing, we were able to create a local version of this dish that is even more delicious than any diner fare. Now we enjoy it often on the weekends, accompanied by bottomless coffee in the comfort of our own kitchen!

1 pound bulk pork sausage
Pinch each of salt and freshly ground
    black pepper
1 teaspoon dried sage
Pinch of freshly grated nutmeg
Pinch of crushed red pepper flakes
    (page 42)

¼ cup all-purpose flour
2½ cups whole milk, plus
    more if desired
6 buttermilk biscuits
    (page 65)

Set a large cast-iron skillet over medium heat and add the sausage, salt, black pepper, sage, nutmeg, and red pepper flakes. Use a wooden spoon to break the sausage up a bit while it cooks. Cook until the meat is no longer pink, 8 to 10 minutes. Taste and adjust the seasonings as needed.

Sprinkle the flour over the sausage and cook, stirring constantly, until it has been absorbed by the fat, 2 to 5 minutes.

Slowly stir in the 2½ cups milk and cook at a bare simmer until the gravy gets thick and the roux coats the back of a spoon. If it is too thick for your liking, add more milk and stir. Taste again for seasonings and adjust as needed.

Gently cut the biscuits in half with a serrated knife and top each half generously with gravy.

Grilled Cheese and Sauerkraut Sandwiches with Farm Stand Tomato Soup

SERVES 4

Localize it

You can use your own homemade tomato sauce recipe instead of the one from me. (You can also use basic canned or freezer tomatoes instead of a tomato sauce, but make sure to taste-test and season a little more if you do.) Use half-and-half in place of the cream. For the grilled cheese sandwich, feel free to use any cheese you'd like!

My mom makes the best grilled cheese. I know that seems like a silly thing to be the best at—but it's true! She gets her bread perfectly fried in the skillet and the cheese evenly melted. In this recipe I use her cooking method but fancy it up a bit with the addition of local sauerkraut. The results are absolutely divine.

FOR THE TOMATO SOUP
1 tablespoon butter
1 medium onion, diced
1 clove of garlic, minced
2 teaspoons dried thyme
½ teaspoon crushed red
   pepper flakes (page 42)
Salt and freshly ground black pepper
½ cup dry red wine
3½ cups Farm Stand Freezer
   Tomato Sauce (page 50)
1½ cups chicken bone broth or veggie
   stock, and more to thin if needed
   (pages 30–31)
½ cup cream

FOR THE GRILLED CHEESE
¼ cup butter
8 slices sourdough bread (page 44)
¼ cup mayonnaise (page 33)
2 tablespoons mustard
8 slices sharp cheddar cheese
½ cup grated cheese
   (a mix of cheddar, Swiss,
   or whatever you fancy!)
1 cup sauerkraut, drained

Make the soup: In a medium-sized pot over medium heat, melt the butter. Stir in the onion and sauté until it is soft and translucent, about 5 minutes. Add the garlic, thyme, red pepper flakes, and salt and black pepper to taste and sauté for an additional 2 minutes. Add the wine and bring to a boil. Reduce the heat to medium and use a wooden spoon to scrape up any brown bits from the bottom.

Stir in the tomato sauce and broth. Bring the soup to a low boil, then reduce the heat to a simmer. Cover and cook for 25 minutes. Pour in the cream and season with additional salt and pepper, if desired.

Meanwhile, make the sandwiches: Heat a large grill pan or skillet over medium-high. Butter 1 side of each slice of bread and spread a thin layer of mayo and mustard on the other side of each slice. Lay 4 bread slices, butter side down, in the pan. Put a slice of cheese on each piece of bread (the mayo side), then sprinkle 2 tablespoons of the grated cheese on top of each piece, followed by a few tablespoons (or to taste) of the sauerkraut.

Add another slice of cheese on top of the sauerkraut and cover it with the remaining 4 bread slices, butter side up. Cook the sandwiches for about 3 minutes on each side, until they are golden brown and the cheese is melted.

Slice the sandwiches in half and serve them with the tomato soup.

Sweet Potato and Bacon Frittata

SERVES 6

Localize it

Any type of dried herb will work in place of the thyme. Don't have local Parmesan? Try an aged cheddar instead. I'm sure ground pork would be a lovely stand-in for the bacon, or you can leave out the bacon and the results will still be delicious—just add a little extra salt to your egg mixture before cooking. Any type of potato would be a delicious alternative to the sweet potatoes.

This is the heartiest of the frittatas in this book, with bacon, potatoes, and cheese to warm up your belly after a cold winter's nap.

8 large eggs
¼ cup cream
¼ cup grated Parmesan
Salt and freshly ground black pepper
6 slices thick-cut bacon, chopped
1 pound sweet potatoes, cut into
  ½-inch chunks

1 medium onion, finely chopped
3 cloves of garlic, finely chopped
2 teaspoons dried thyme
¼ teaspoon crushed red
  pepper flakes (page 42)
3 ounces goat cheese

Set an oven rack 5 inches from the heat and preheat the broiler.

In a large bowl, whisk together the eggs, cream, cheese, and a hefty pinch each of salt and black pepper.

In a 10-inch cast-iron skillet over medium heat, cook the bacon, stirring often, until it is crisp. Transfer it with a slotted spoon to a small bowl, then pour off all but about 2 tablespoons of the fat, reserving the poured-out fat in a small bowl or mason jar.

Add the sweet potatoes to the skillet and sauté them over medium-high heat until golden, about 3 minutes. Give the potatoes a good stir, cover the pan, and cook for 2 to 3 minutes longer until the potatoes are just tender. Transfer them with a slotted spoon to a medium bowl.

Add 1 tablespoon of the reserved bacon fat to the skillet and sauté the onion, garlic, thyme, and red pepper flakes over medium-high heat until the onion is softened, about 4 minutes.

Add the potatoes and half the bacon back to the skillet, spreading evenly.

Pour the egg mixture over the vegetables and cook the frittata over medium-high heat, lifting the cooked egg around the edges with a rubber spatula to let the uncooked eggs flow underneath, 2 to 3 minutes. Reduce the heat to medium and cook, giving the pan a shake now and again until the eggs are mostly set but the center is still slightly jiggly, 3 to 5 minutes more.

Dollop the goat cheese around the frittata and sprinkle it with the remaining bacon.

Place the frittata under the broiler until the cheese is browned and the center is set, 2 to 3 minutes (watch carefully, as you can quickly overcook the frittata).

Cut into wedges and serve.

Simple Roasted Pork Shoulder

SERVES 6 TO 8

Localize it

Swap garlic or a diced onion for shallots. Use any dried herbs you'd like.

Everyone should have a simple pork shoulder recipe in their back pocket for the long winter months. This recipe serves a crowd and is so darn simple to prepare that you just can't go wrong. Serve it with any of your favorite side dishes (it's particularly delicious with roasted cauliflower with bread crumbs, page 103, or my Apple, Kohlrabi, and Hazelnut Slaw, page 107) Leftovers come in handy for sandwiches, tacos, or stews during the week.

3 tablespoons olive oil
3 tablespoons chopped garlic
1 tablespoon dried thyme
Generous pinch of salt and freshly ground black pepper
1 (4-pound) bone-in pork shoulder

2 teaspoons dried thyme
¼ teaspoon crushed red pepper flakes (page 42)
Flaky sea salt, to taste

Preheat the oven to 425°F.

In a small bowl, mix together the olive oil, garlic, thyme, salt, and pepper.

Using a pastry brush, or your bare hands, spread the mixture all over the pork shoulder.

Set a rack in a roasting pan and place the meat on it. Roast for 25 minutes, then reduce the heat to 325°F. Continue to roast for about 4 hours or until the pork is cooked through and tender. (A meat thermometer inserted into the shoulder should read 180°F, which is the ideal temperature for pulling the pork apart.)

Remove the pork from the oven and let it stand until it is cool enough to handle, about 30 minutes. Shred the pork using two forks and sprinkle with flaky sea salt to taste.

Macaroni and Cheese

SERVES 6

Localize it

Any type of whole milk (goat or cow) and any type of hard cheese that you can find will work. I think a Swiss would be awesome for a different twist or even a mix of cheddar and Swiss.

While I was editing this cookbook, my neighbor brought over a macaroni and cheese dish that knocked our socks off. Her two secret ingredients were bacon (from her own pigs) and a pinch of nutmeg. Sounds a little strange, I know, but we absolutely loved it. This dish still evokes the nostalgia of comfort food but has a bit of a more sophisticated twist. Bonus: It's easy to make with local ingredients and is a great way to try out the products of artisanal cheesemakers in your area.

FOR THE MACARONI AND CHEESE
1 pound elbow pasta
4 slices thick-cut bacon, roughly chopped
3 tablespoons unsalted butter
¼ teaspoon ground nutmeg
¼ cup all-purpose flour
4 cups whole milk
1 clove of garlic, finely minced
½ teaspoon crushed red pepper flakes (page 42)

Salt and freshly ground black pepper
3 cups sharp cheddar cheese, grated

FOR THE TOPPING
1 cup coarse bread crumbs (page 47)
¼ cup melted butter or olive oil
¼ teaspoon dried parsley
¼ cup grated Parmesan cheese
Salt and freshly ground black pepper

Preheat the oven to 425°F.

Make the mac and cheese: In a large pot of salted boiling water, cook the pasta until it's barely al dente. (It's going to continue to cook in the oven.) Drain and set aside.

In a large, heavy-bottom pot, cook the bacon over medium heat, stirring often until lightly browned. Remove the bacon to a paper-towel-lined plate to drain. Pour out all but 1 tablespoon of the bacon fat into a mason jar or bowl and reserve for another use.

Add the butter to the pot with the reserved bacon fat over medium heat. Add the nutmeg and stir well. Once the butter is slightly foamy, whisk in the flour and cook, whisking constantly, until the mixture is just starting to turn a light golden brown, about 4 minutes. Slowly whisk in the milk and stir constantly to avoid clumping. Add the garlic and red pepper flakes and season with salt and black pepper to taste. Bring the mixture to a simmer, continuing to whisk constantly to make sure the flour is fully incorporated.

Add the grated cheese and whisk to blend until the cheese is completely melted. Season the sauce again with salt and pepper and add the cooked pasta and reserved bacon. Stir to coat the noodles well. (The sauce will be thick, but it will thin as it cooks.)

Make the topping: In a medium bowl, combine the bread crumbs, melted butter, dried parsley, and Parmesan. Season with salt and pepper and mix well.

Transfer the macaroni and cheese mixture to a 9-by-13-inch baking dish and scatter the topping evenly over it. Place the dish on a rimmed baking sheet. Bake until the macaroni and cheese is bubbling and the bread crumbs are evenly golden brown, 25 to 30 minutes.

Let cool slightly before serving.

Spaghetti Bolognese with Summer Tomatoes

SERVES 4

Localize it

Use any ground meat you have: turkey, pork, venison, lamb, or chicken. Any type of local freshly grated hard cheese will work, too: Parmesan, cheddar, Swiss.

Meals don't get much easier than this classic Italian-American staple. For us, winter is all about these kinds of dishes that are a little bit heavier on the starch and protein than we may normally eat, but feel essential and comforting to our bodies after a day of shoveling snow and planting seedlings in the chilly greenhouse. A bowl of this pasta is best enjoyed cuddled up under a blanket with a glass of your favorite wine.

½ pound spaghetti
Up to 4 tablespoons unsalted butter or olive oil
1 pound ground beef
1 large onion, finely chopped
1 teaspoon dried thyme
Dash of crushed red pepper flakes (page 42)

2 cloves of garlic, finely chopped
Salt and freshly ground black pepper
2½ cups Farm Stand Freezer Tomato Sauce (page 50)
Freshly grated cheese for serving

Bring a large pot of lightly salted water to a boil. Add the pasta and cook until al dente, 8 to 10 minutes. Drain the pasta, add a little butter or oil, toss it, and set it aside.

In a large, deep skillet over medium heat, brown the meat, using a wooden spoon to break it up a bit, and cook until it is no longer pink, about 3 minutes. Use a slotted spoon to remove the meat from the pan and set it aside.

If the skillet is super greasy from the meat, add only a pat of butter, but if it's pretty clean, add about 2 tablespoons. Then add the chopped onion, thyme, and red pepper flakes. Cook for about 5 minutes, stirring occasionally, until the onions are softened. Add the garlic and season with salt and black pepper. Cook for an additional minute, until the garlic is fragrant. Add the meat and tomato sauce to the pan and bring to a simmer. Simmer over low heat for about 20 minutes.

Add the drained pasta to the meat sauce. Use tongs to toss it together until the pasta is well coated.

Serve the pasta with freshly grated cheese.

Ham Steaks with Glazed Apples and Honey Mustard–Port Sauce

SERVES 4

Localize it

You can use pears in place of apples. It would also be wonderful with chopped dried fruit such as cherries, apricots, or figs. They'll become melt-in-your-mouth tender after you cook them in a little butter!

There is just something special about the combination of ham and apples. And when you toss in a sweet and slightly tangy sauce made with honey mustard and port, the results are absolutely mouthwatering. I posted this recipe on my blog a few years back, and it got such rave reviews that I knew I had to create a local version for this book!

2 (1-pound) ham steaks, about ½ inch thick, patted dry
2 cups apple cider
3 tablespoons honey
2 tablespoons Dijon mustard
Freshly ground black pepper
½ cup ruby port

1 tablespoon unsalted butter
1 apple, very thinly sliced (any variety of apple will work, but I like choosing a slightly tart apple like Granny Smith)
8 sage leaves

Preheat the oven to 350°F.

In a large baking dish, place the ham steaks side by side (it's okay if they overlap a bit) and pour in 1 cup of the apple cider.

In a small bowl, whisk together 1½ tablespoons of the honey and the Dijon mustard. Spread this over the ham steaks and sprinkle them with pepper. Bake the ham steaks for about 40 minutes.

Meanwhile, in a medium-sized saucepan, combine the remaining 1 cup of apple cider with the remaining 1½ tablespoons honey and the port. Bring the mixture to a boil, reduce the heat, and simmer until the sauce has reduced to roughly ½ cup and thickened up a bit, about 15 minutes.

In a medium-sized frying pan over medium heat, melt the butter. Add the apple slices in a single layer and cook until they are crisp-tender, about 1 minute. Flip the apples and continue to cook them for about 45 seconds (you don't want them to become mushy). Transfer the apples to a plate.

Add the sage leaves to the same pan and cook until they turn bright green. Set them aside with the apples.

Slice the ham steaks in half and place a piece on each plate. Drizzle them with the sauce and top them with the apples and fried sage leaves.

Lazy Chickadee Pâté

6 TO 8 SERVINGS

Localize it

Use duck or rabbit liver in place of chicken. Swap the sherry out for any other fortified wine.

I used to think of pâté as fancy food for classy folks. But this amazingly rich, decadent spread is made with chicken liver, which is actually very inexpensive. This is my sister-in-law's recipe, and it is hands down one of the tastiest condiments I've ever had the pleasure of spreading onto a piece of toast. Whip up a batch of this pâté and freeze some for later—it comes in handy for entertaining. Serve it with homemade pickles or jam, a baguette, and a bottle of wine, and you will impress any guest!

½ cup (1 stick) butter
1 pound chicken livers
Salt and freshly ground black pepper
2 strips bacon, diced
1 small onion, sliced
1 apple, cored and cubed
Handful of fresh thyme
½ cup chopped parsley

2 cloves of garlic, minced
1 cinnamon stick
¼ cup water
¼ cup sherry
1 tablespoon balsamic vinegar
¾ teaspoon freshly grated nutmeg
Olive oil for topping the jars

In a large, deep skillet over medium-high heat, melt 4 tablespoons of the butter. Season the livers with salt and pepper, add them to the skillet, and cook, turning once, until they are just cooked through (the liver may still be slightly pink inside), about 4 minutes per side. Remove them from the skillet and set them aside.

Add the bacon to the skillet and stir until it is cooked but not crispy. Then add the onion and season with salt and pepper. Cook, stirring, until the onion is translucent, about 5 minutes. Add the apple, thyme, parsley, garlic, cinnamon stick, and ¼ cup water. Cover and cook, stirring occasionally and adding water as necessary to prevent burning, until the apple pieces are soft and easily pierced with the tip of a knife.

Add the sherry to deglaze the pan and allow it to reduce by about half.

Remove the thyme sprigs and cinnamon sticks from the skillet and discard them.

Cut the remaining 4 tablespoons of butter into small cubes. Transfer the contents of the skillet to a food processor with the chicken livers, vinegar, nutmeg, and cut butter. Process until the pâté is very smooth. Season with salt and pepper.

Strain the pâté by using a spatula to push it through a fine-mesh sieve.

Transfer the pâté to a glass jar, small mason jars, or Tupperware; drizzle the top with a little oil and place in the fridge for up to seven days or in the freezer for up to six months.

Winter Squash Wedges with Gorgonzola Butter and Hazelnuts

SERVES 4

Localize it

You could sub in roasted carrots or roasted beets for the winter squash. Try using any local nut or seed in place of the hazelnuts. And a nice local blue cheese is a great substitute for the Gorgonzola.

Life hasn't been the same since Deborah Madison introduced me to Gorgonzola butter in her classic cookbook *Vegetable Literacy*. It's a lovely condiment to jazz up any meat or vegetable dish, and it makes these winter squash wedges something special. Any winter squash variety will work—delicata, butternut, acorn, kabocha, etc.—and you don't need to bother peeling it (unless you're sensitive to the skin), because most squash varieties have edible skins that become quite tender once cooked. I like to smear a thin layer of the butter onto a plate and place the squash on top so that with each bite I get a little taste of the incredible cheesy, buttery spread.

FOR THE GORGONZOLA BUTTER

1 clove of garlic, minced
Sea salt
3 tablespoons unsalted butter, room temperature
3 tablespoons Gorgonzola or any blue cheese

FOR THE WINTER SQUASH

1½ pounds winter squash, cut into ½-inch-thick wedges
2 to 3 tablespoons melted butter
Sea salt
Minced parsley for serving
2 tablespoons toasted and crushed hazelnuts
Freshly ground black pepper

Make the Gorgonzola butter: In a medium-sized bowl, pound the garlic and a hefty pinch of salt with the back of a spoon until a paste forms. Add the butter and cheese and mix until well incorporated. Set aside.

Make the squash: Heat a cast-iron skillet over medium-high heat and brush the squash wedges with a little melted butter. Add the squash to the skillet and cook, undisturbed, for a few minutes. Once the squash begins to brown up a bit, turn the wedges and continue to cook, turning them every few minutes, until they are tender, about 25 minutes. Season with a pinch of salt.

Spoon a thin layer of the Gorgonzola butter onto a platter and top it with the squash. Sprinkle with the minced parsley, hazelnuts, and freshly ground black pepper.

Oxtail and Sweet Potato Stew

SERVES 6

Localize it

Any winter squash would work well in place of sweet potatoes. Add a rutabaga or turnip in place of the parsnips.

I wrote this book while I was pregnant, and my midwife friend encouraged me to test recipes with organ meat and bone broths to give my body the protein and collagen it needed to build a new life. She slipped me this recipe for a rustic oxtail stew, which is hearty, nourishing, and delicious, whether you're eating for one or two!

3 pounds oxtails with separated joints
Salt and freshly ground black pepper
Cooking fat (page xv)
1 large yellow or red onion, finely chopped
3 whole cloves of garlic, peels still on
2 cups beef bone broth or stock (pages 30–31)

2 cups dry red wine
1 bay leaf
Hefty pinch of dried thyme
2 pounds sweet potatoes, cut into 1-inch pieces (no need to peel)
2 parsnips, cut into 1-inch pieces (no need to peel)
Minced parsley for serving

Pat the oxtails dry with paper towels. Sprinkle them all over with salt and pepper.

In a large Dutch oven over medium-high, heat 1 tablespoon of cooking fat.

Working in batches, and not crowding the pan, sear the oxtails on all sides until they are golden brown. Use tongs to remove the oxtails to a plate.

Add the chopped onion. Cook for a few minutes, until it is translucent.

Add the oxtails back to the pan with the onion. Then add the whole garlic cloves, stock, and wine. Add the bay leaf, thyme, and a hefty pinch of salt. Bring the mixture to a simmer and then reduce the heat to low. Cover and cook for 2 hours.

Last, add the chopped sweet potatoes and parsnips to the pot. Cover the pot and cook until the meat and vegetables are tender, about 1 hour more.

Remove the bay leaf from the pot and ladle the stew into bowls. Sprinkle it with minced parsley.

Baked Apple Oatmeal

SERVES 6

Note

You can also prepare this in an 8- or 9-inch baking dish. The cook time will be 50 to 60 minutes.

Localize it

Any type of dried fruit or nut would work well here—dried blueberries or cherries, for example. You could also swap in pears for the apples.

This is a great recipe to make on a Sunday afternoon for easy breakfasts all week long—just scoop some oatmeal into a bowl and reheat. It's a breeze to prepare and is chock-full of warming spices and comforting flavors. I love the crunchy exterior the oatmeal gets from baking—it creates a texture that almost feels like dessert. Pair it with a cup of coffee, and you're all set to tackle the day!

2 cups old-fashioned rolled oats (not instant)
½ cup honey
1 cup walnuts
½ cup dried cranberries
1 teaspoon baking powder
2 teaspoons ground cinnamon
¼ teaspoon ground nutmeg
½ teaspoon salt
2 large eggs
2 cups milk
¼ cup unsalted butter, melted, plus more for greasing the dish
2 small apples, cored, and cut into ½-inch chunks (about 1½ cups)

Preheat the oven to 325°F.

In a medium bowl, combine the oats, honey, ½ cup of the nuts, the cranberries, baking powder, cinnamon, nutmeg, and salt. Mix well.

In another medium bowl, lightly beat the eggs with a whisk, then whisk in the milk until well combined.

Add the milk mixture to the oat mixture, along with the melted butter, and mix well.

Grease 6 individual ramekins with butter.

Scatter the apples evenly on the bottom of the ramekins. Pour the oatmeal mixture over the top and spread it evenly. Sprinkle the remaining ½ cup nuts on top. Bake until the tops are golden and the oats are set, 35 to 45 minutes.

Serve warm or at room temperature.

Rustic Lamb Stew

SERVES 6 TO 8

Localize it

You can try this with beef, venison, goat, or elk. Any mix of dried herbs will be just fine. Try swapping the carrots and parsnips for sweet potatoes and rutabagas.

I really enjoy cooking with lamb—it's rich and nourishing, and every time I use it, I'm inspired to make more lamb recipes because the flavor is so unique and satisfying. This is the kind of stew you make on a cold, snowy winter afternoon when the woodstove is crackling and you've stayed in your long johns all day long.

4 pounds lamb stew meat or boneless lamb shoulder, cut into 2-inch chunks
2 to 3 tablespoons cooking fat (page xv)
2 large onions, roughly chopped
4 cloves of garlic, minced
3 teaspoons dried thyme
2 teaspoons dried parsley
Salt
Freshly ground black pepper
1 teaspoon ground allspice

3 medium carrots, cut into 1-inch pieces
2 medium parsnips, cut into 1-inch pieces
¼ cup all-purpose flour
¼ cup tomato paste (page 39)
1 cup dry red wine (we used a Pinot Noir)
4 small potatoes, cubed
3 to 4 cups beef or lamb stock (page 31)

Preheat the oven to 325°F.

Pat the lamb dry with paper towels. In a 6- to 8-quart Dutch oven or soup pot over medium-high, heat 1 tablespoon of the cooking fat until hot. Add the lamb, in three separate batches, and cook 6 to 8 minutes per batch or until browned on all sides, adding more cooking fat if necessary. Transfer the browned lamb to a medium bowl and set aside.

Reduce the heat to medium. Add about 1 tablespoon of the cooking fat to the pot and stir in the onions, garlic, thyme, parsley, a hefty pinch of salt, a few grinds of black pepper, and the allspice. Cook for about 1 minute or until the onions and garlic are nicely coated in the herb mixture and it's becoming fragrant. Add the carrots and parsnips and cook for about 8 minutes longer or until the vegetables are browned and tender, stirring occasionally. Stir in the flour, and cook for 2 minutes. Add the tomato paste, then the wine, and bring the mixture to a boil, stirring until the browned bits are loosened from the bottom of the pot, about 5 minutes. Return the lamb with its juices to the pot and add the potatoes. Pour in the stock and bring to a boil.

Cover the Dutch oven and bake for 1 hour and 30 minutes or until the meat is fork-tender. Skim and discard any fat from the liquid.

Serve warm with a hunk of sourdough bread (page 44).

Wine-Braised Pork Shoulder

Localize it

This would be lovely made with a pot roast, elk roast, or venison roast. Using a bone-in pork shoulder gives this great flavor, but if you can't find bone-in, use a 3½- to 4-pound boneless shoulder, and note that the cooking time will be slightly less. Any dried herb will work well here.

This take on pork shoulder is bursting with deep flavors that develop while the meat slowly cooks. Aside from a little chopping and basting, the recipe is pretty hands-off, so it's a good one for entertaining. Serve it with a side of mashed potatoes, or Roasted Cauliflower with Bread Crumbs (page 103) for a perfect winter meal.

1 (4½-pound) bone-in pork shoulder
1 tablespoon dried basil
1 tablespoon dried thyme
1 tablespoon dried parsley
1 tablespoon salt
2 teaspoons freshly ground black pepper

2 large red onions, thinly sliced
2 cups dry red wine (We used a Cabernet.)
1 bunch of parsley, finely chopped

Preheat the oven to 325°F.

Pat the pork shoulder dry with paper towels. In a small bowl, combine all the dried herbs, salt, and pepper.

In the bottom of a large Dutch oven, layer the onions. Place the roast fat side down on top of the onions and sprinkle in half of the spice mixture. Use your hands to rub it evenly over the pork. Flip the pork over so the fat side is up and rub in the remainder of the spice mixture. Pour in the wine and cover.

Transfer the Dutch oven to the oven and cook for 3½ to 4½ hours, basting the pork every hour or so, until the meat is tender and falling off the bone and an instant-read thermometer inserted in the thickest part registers about 180°F.

When the meat is tender, remove the shoulder from the pot and wait for it to cool slightly. Use two forks to shred the meat.

Skim any fat off the juices in the pot and then strain the liquid into a saucepan. Transfer about half the onions to the saucepan with the liquid and place the remainder back in the Dutch oven. Bring the mixture in the saucepan to a low boil. Reduce the heat and simmer until it is slightly reduced, about 8 minutes. Carefully transfer the mixture to a high-speed blender and puree until smooth.

Return the shredded meat to the Dutch oven and drizzle in the sauce. Toss the meat and onions to coat with the sauce and keep it warm over low heat on the stovetop until ready to serve. Ladle it into bowls and garnish with a sprinkling of fresh parsley.

Creamed Peas and Onions

SERVES 8 TO 10

Localize it

Any type of onion will work here, just slice larger onions into quarters. If you didn't freeze any sweet peas, you can try this with corn for a totally different, yet equally delicious alternative.

This is an old-fashioned recipe typically served around the holidays—but also a great excuse to dip into the freezer and fetch produce from the previous spring. Between the brought-back-to-life peas, tender onions, and sweet cream, this comforting dish is also a celebration of local ingredients. I like to spoon it over toasted sourdough bread (page 44), but it's equally good served with mashed potatoes or a grilled steak (page 223).

2 large yellow onions, peeled, trimmed and quartered (about 1 pound)
3 tablespoons unsalted butter
Salt
1 teaspoon honey

2 tablespoons all-purpose flour
2 cups whole milk
¼ teaspoon freshly grated nutmeg
Freshly ground black pepper
2 pounds frozen peas, thawed

Place the onions in a large skillet. Add enough water to half cover the onions. Add 1 tablespoon of the butter, a hefty pinch of salt, and the honey. Cook over medium-high heat, stirring occasionally, until the liquid has mostly evaporated and the onions are golden brown, about 12 minutes. Transfer the onions to a large plate. It's okay if there are still some bits of the onions in the pan.

Reduce the heat to medium and melt the remaining 2 tablespoons butter in the skillet; add the flour and whisk to combine. Cook, stirring occasionally and scraping up browned bits from the bottom of the pan, for 1 minute. Whisk in the milk ¼ cup at a time. Cook, stirring constantly, until the mixture is thickened and bubbly. Stir in another pinch of salt, the nutmeg, and the pepper. Add the peas and onions; stir until heated through.

Serve hot, spooned over toast or baked potatoes, or as a side to steak.

Creamy Celeriac Soup with Pancetta and Toasted Hazelnuts

SERVES 4 TO 6

Localize it

Use a rutabaga or turnip in place of the celeriac. Any nut or seed will be great in the topping.

This soup is one of the best ways to celebrate an often overlooked vegetable—the mighty celeriac (aka celery root)! It's a root vegetable and a lovely addition to soups, stews, and braises, becoming slightly sweet and creamy when cooked. It tastes even better with the salty pancetta and toasted hazelnut topping.

4 ounces pancetta or thick-cut bacon, chopped
1 to 2 teaspoons cooking fat (page xv)
1 medium yellow onion, chopped
2 large cloves of garlic, minced
1 teaspoon dried thyme
¼ teaspoon crushed red pepper flakes (page 42)
1 bay leaf

2 pounds celeriac, peeled and cut into ½-inch chunks
4 cups chicken bone broth or stock, plus additional to thin the soup (pages 30–31)
Salt and freshly ground black pepper
½ cup heavy cream
¼ cup hazelnuts
¼ cup chopped parsley
Olive oil for drizzling

In a large heavy-bottom pan or soup pot over medium-high heat, cook the pancetta for about 3 minutes on each side until crisp. Transfer it to a paper-towel-lined plate to drain.

Melt the cooking fat in the same pan and add the onion. Sauté for about 5 minutes, stirring often. Add the garlic, thyme, red pepper flakes, bay leaf, and celeriac chunks. Cook for about 2 minutes longer. Pour in the stock and add a pinch of salt and pepper. Bring to a boil, then reduce the heat to medium-low and simmer until the vegetables are tender, about 25 minutes.

Remove the bay leaf, stir in the heavy cream, then transfer the soup to a high-speed blender and puree on high until completely smooth and creamy (depending on the size of your blender, you may need to do this in batches; alternatively, you can use an immersion blender, but the soup won't be as smooth).

Return the soup to the pot and keep it on low. Give it a taste test and season it with additional salt and pepper if needed. If the soup seems too thick, add a touch more stock or water.

Meanwhile, heat a small dry skillet over medium-high heat. Add the hazelnuts and cook until they are lightly toasted on all sides, 5 to 8 minutes. Shake the pan often to ensure the nuts cook evenly. Remove them from the pan, and when they are cool enough to handle, roughly chop them.

Ladle the soup into bowls and top each portion with the pancetta, hazelnuts, and parsley. Drizzle with a tiny bit of olive oil and season to taste with salt and pepper.

Sheet Pan Sausages with Cabbage and Potatoes

SERVES 4

Localize it

Try turnips, rutabagas, or even sweet potatoes for the potatoes. Swap chopped romaine for the cabbage. Any nut or seed oil can replace the olive oil.

Sausage, potatoes, and cabbage have always been one of my favorite food combinations, and this meal does not disappoint. This recipe is super low-maintenance and great for feeding a family. Save yourself another dish to wash by simply transferring the sheet pan from the oven to the table and letting everyone choose what they want to put on their plates. It doesn't get much easier than that!

FOR THE SAUSAGE, CABBAGE, AND POTATOES

1 pound small potatoes, sliced in half (about the size of a Ping-Pong ball)

1 head cabbage (about 1 pound), cut into 4 wedges

¼ cup olive oil, plus more for drizzling

Salt and freshly ground black pepper

4 Italian sausages (about 1 pound total), each pierced with a fork in a few places

FOR THE DRESSING

1 clove of garlic, minced

Salt

Freshly ground black pepper

1 tablespoon coarse-grain mustard

1 tablespoon red wine vinegar

2 teaspoons honey

¼ cup extra-virgin olive oil

Preheat the oven to 425°F.

Make the vegetables and sausage: On a rimmed baking sheet, toss the potatoes and cabbage with the oil and salt and pepper. Roast the vegetables for about 15 minutes. Remove them from the oven, toss the potatoes and flip the cabbage, then arrange the sausages on the pan. Drizzle with a bit more oil and place the pan back in the oven until sausages are cooked through and the cabbage and potatoes are browned and tender, about 30 minutes. Flip the sausages and give the pan a good shake halfway through cooking.

Make the dressing: In a small bowl, whisk together all the dressing ingredients until they are well combined. Taste for seasonings and adjust as needed.

Remove the sheet pan from the oven, drizzle with the dressing, and serve warm.

Meatloaf with Mushroom Gravy

SERVES 6

Localize it

Use any type of ground meat (chicken, duck, turkey) and any variety of mushrooms (wild or cultivated).

This is one of those incredibly easy meatloaf recipes that's still bursting with lots of flavor. The meatloaf itself is basic, without the addition of the usual suspects (onions, celery, carrots, ketchup). I left it simple for a reason: Meatloaf is the perfect vehicle for this mushroom gravy. And while any ground meat will work here, I like to use a mixture of beef and pork, the latter of which adds a bit of extra fat and moisture.

FOR THE MEATLOAF
Olive oil, for greasing the pan
1 pound ground beef
½ pound ground pork
1 egg, beaten
1 cup whole milk
1 tablespoon red wine vinegar
1¼ teaspoons salt
Freshly ground black pepper
1 teaspoon dried thyme
1 cup bread crumbs (page 47)

FOR THE MUSHROOM GRAVY
3 tablespoons unsalted butter
1 pound mixed mushrooms, diced
2 large shallots, finely chopped
 (about ½ cup)
Salt and freshly ground black pepper
1 teaspoon dried thyme
2 tablespoons all-purpose flour
1¼ cups beef stock (page 31),
 plus more to thin if needed
½ cup heavy cream

Make the meatloaf: Preheat the oven to 350°F. Lightly grease a standard 8-by-4-inch loaf pan with olive oil and set aside.

In a large mixing bowl, combine the beef, pork, and egg. Add the milk, stirring to combine. Gently stir in the vinegar, salt, pepper to taste, thyme, and bread crumbs. Pat the mixture down into the oiled loaf pan. Bake for 1 hour or until the meat is browned and the inside is cooked through.

Meanwhile, make the gravy: In a large, heavy-bottom cast-iron pan, heat the butter until it foams. Add the diced mushrooms and cook them over high heat, stirring occasionally, until they start to release their liquid and shrink down a bit, about 5 minutes. Add the shallots, salt, pepper, and thyme and continue to cook until the mushrooms begin to brown, the shallots are translucent, and the mixture is fragrant, 3 to 5 minutes. Sprinkle the flour over the mushrooms and stir well to evenly coat. Reduce the heat to medium and continue to cook, stirring occasionally, for about 2 minutes. Stir in the stock. Whisk the mixture well to incorporate the flour. Add a splash more stock or water if the mixture seems too thick, then reduce the heat to low and stir in the cream. Taste and season with salt and pepper as needed.

Slice the meatloaf and serve it with the gravy.

Fennel & Hazelnut Gratin

SERVES 6

Localize it

Use any dried or fresh herb that you can get your hands on. Any nut or seed will work well for the topping.

Fennel is a vegetable people tend to love or hate, but this dish is a great way to win over fennel skeptics. Once roasted, its anise-like flavor mellows out quite a bit and turns sweet and earthy. I like to top this casserole with a hazelnut crumble for a lovely crunch and nutty flavor that pairs perfectly with the fennel.

3 medium fennel bulbs, trimmed (save some fronds for garnish)
½ cup chicken stock (page 31)
⅓ cup dry white wine
Salt and freshly ground black pepper

½ teaspoon dried thyme
5 tablespoons unsalted butter
¾ cup toasted hazelnuts, roughly chopped
1 cup freshly grated cheddar cheese
¼ cup finely chopped parsley

Preheat the oven to 375°F.

Cut the bulbs into quarters, then into approximately 2-inch wedges. Discard the woody cores. Arrange the wedges, cut sides up, in a single layer in a large casserole dish.

Pour the stock and wine over the fennel, then sprinkle it with salt, pepper, and thyme. Dice 2 tablespoons of the butter and use it to dot the fennel. Cover the dish tightly with aluminum foil and bake for 35 to 45 minutes or until the fennel is tender. Remove it from the oven, use tongs to flip the fennel, and raise the oven temperature to 425°F.

Meanwhile, melt the remaining 3 tablespoons butter and mix it in a medium-sized bowl with the hazelnuts, cheese, parsley, and a pinch of salt and pepper.

Uncover the fennel, sprinkle the topping evenly over it, and return it to the oven. Bake uncovered for 30 minutes or until the topping is browned.

Serve immediately.

Shepherd's Pie

Localize it

Any root vegetable or winter squash will work beautifully here. Try leeks in place of onions, or add some frozen green beans in place of peas. Any mix of dried herbs will be just fine.

Shepherd's pie is an economical stick-to-your-bones kind of meal. It's easy to source many of these ingredients locally in the dead of winter. It's the kind of dish that pairs best with a woodstove, previously worn and wet clothes hanging out to dry, and a freshly uncorked bottle of red wine.

1 pound ground lamb
1 tablespoon cooking fat (page xv)
1 large onion, chopped
3 large cloves of garlic, minced
2 large carrots, chopped
1 large parsnip, chopped
1 cup beef or chicken broth (page 30)
½ cup red wine
1 tablespoon tomato paste (page 39)

1 teaspoon dried rosemary
1 teaspoon dried thyme
1 teaspoon dried parsley
½ teaspoon crushed red pepper flakes (page 42)
1 cup frozen peas
2 pounds potatoes, cut into chunks
6 tablespoons unsalted butter
½ cup plus 1 tablespoon whole milk
Salt
1 egg

Preheat the oven to 375°F.

In a large, heavy-bottom cast-iron pan over medium-high, cook the lamb, using a wooden spoon to break up the meat a bit, until browned all over and no longer pink. With a slotted spoon, remove the meat from the pan and set aside on a paper-towel-lined plate to drain. Add the cooking fat, then add the onion, garlic, carrots, and parsnip. Cook until the vegetables begin to soften, 8 to 10 minutes.

Add the meat back to the pan along with the broth, wine, tomato paste, dried herbs, and red pepper flakes. Simmer until the liquid reduces a bit and the mixture thickens, about 10 minutes, then add the peas. Remove from the heat.

Place the potatoes in a medium-sized pot with salted water to cover and bring it to a boil. Cook until the potatoes are tender, 18 to 20 minutes; drain.

Mash the potatoes with the butter, ½ cup of the milk, and salt.

In a small bowl, whisk together the egg and the remaining 1 tablespoon milk.

Spread the potatoes over the meat-and-veggie mixture, brush with the egg wash, then crosshatch the top with a fork.

Bake until the shepherd's pie is golden, 30 to 35 minutes.

Pork, Butternut, and Bean Stew

SERVES 8 TO 10

Localize it

You can swap beef for the pork. Any type of winter squash will work well—pumpkin, acorn, delicata, kabocha.

The flavor of this stew is phenomenal: The tomatoes, smoked paprika, and red wine give it a nice richness without making it too heavy. The meat melts in your mouth, and the beans add a lovely texture. When a stew like this is simmering in your kitchen and the whole house begins to smell amazing, it's motivation enough to call over the neighbors to share a meal.

FOR THE BEANS
¼ pound dry white or pinto beans
Pinch of salt
¼ teaspoon freshly ground black pepper
1 bay leaf
1 large clove of garlic, smashed
¼ of a large yellow or red onion, peeled

FOR THE STEW
2 tablespoons cooking fat (page xv)
3 pounds pork shoulder, cut into 1½-inch cubes
Salt
1 large onion, diced
3 large cloves of garlic, finely chopped
2 tablespoons tomato paste (page 39)
½ teaspoon smoked paprika
1½ teaspoons dried thyme
½ cup dry red wine
1 pint jar diced tomatoes with juices (or one 16-ounce can store-bought tomatoes)
2½ cups homemade or low-sodium pork, chicken, or vegetable stock (page 31)
1 bay leaf
2 pounds butternut squash, cut into ½-inch cubes (about 3 cups)

Preheat the oven to 350°F.

Make the beans: Put the beans in a large bowl, cover them with cold water, and soak them for at least 7 hours. Drain the beans, then rinse and put them in a medium-sized saucepan. Cover them with at least 2 inches of water and add the salt, pepper, bay leaf, garlic, and onion. Bring the mixture to a boil, give it a stir, and lower the heat to a gentle simmer. Cook until just tender, 30 to 40 minutes. Drain the beans, removing and discarding the garlic and onion. Reserve the bay leaf. Set the beans aside.

Make the stew: In a medium-sized Dutch oven over medium-high, heat 1 tablespoon of the cooking fat. Season half the pork well with salt and add it to the pot. Brown the cubes on all sides, about 5 minutes total. Remove the pork to a plate with a slotted spoon and repeat with the rest of the meat, adding more cooking fat as needed.

Reduce the heat to medium-low and add the onion and a pinch of salt. Cook, stirring frequently, until softened, about 5 minutes. Add the garlic and cook for another minute, until fragrant. Stir in the tomato paste, paprika, and thyme. Cook for another 2 minutes. Add the wine and bring the mixture to a boil. Reduce the heat to medium low and cook until most of the liquid has evaporated, scraping up any brown bits as needed.

Add the tomatoes, stock, reserved bay leaf, and a pinch of salt, as well as the browned pork and any accumulated juices. Stir well and bring the stew to a boil over medium-high heat. Reduce the heat to medium, and when the stew comes to a simmer, cover the pot and transfer it to the oven. Cook for 1½ hours.

Add the cooked beans and the cubed squash to the pot and gently stir. Return the stew to the oven for another 30 to 45 minutes, until the meat and the squash are fork-tender. Taste and adjust the seasonings if necessary.

Serve warm with toasted sourdough bread (page 44) for dunking.

Pan-Seared Steak with Red Wine Sauce

SERVES 4 TO 6

Localize it

Use any cut of steak here; bone-in or boneless will both work just fine. Any fresh or dried herb will be lovely.

My grandma made the best steak around. Whether she was searing it, grilling it, or baking it, with minimal ingredients and not a lot of fuss, she always managed to nail it. This recipe makes me think of her. The steak is tender and juicy, and the flavors meld together wonderfully to create a simple and satisfying main course.

2 (8-ounce) top-sirloin steaks, trimmed
Salt and freshly ground black pepper
1 tablespoon cooking fat (page xv)
1 small shallot, minced
1 tablespoon minced fresh rosemary, or 1½ teaspoons dried
Hefty pinch crushed red pepper flakes

½ cup full-bodied red wine (like a Syrah or Merlot)
½ cup bone broth, beef stock, or veggie stock (pages 30–31)
1½ teaspoons unsalted butter or ghee
1 teaspoon Dijon mustard
Flaky sea salt

Pat the steaks dry and sprinkle them evenly with salt and pepper, using a hefty pinch of each.

In a large cast-iron skillet over high, heat the cooking fat. Add the steaks to the pan and cook them for 4 minutes per side (for medium-rare) or to the desired doneness. Remove the steaks from the pan and let them sit for about 5 minutes.

Reduce the heat under the skillet to medium-high. Add the shallot, rosemary, and red pepper flakes. Sauté for 1 minute. Add the wine and cook until most of the liquid evaporates, about 3 minutes. Add the stock and cook until the sauce reduces a bit and thickens up, 3 to 5 minutes longer. Remove the pan from the heat and stir in the butter and mustard; taste the sauce and adjust the seasonings.

Cut the steaks across the grain into thin pieces and drizzle with the sauce. Sprinkle the meat with a few pinches of flaky sea salt and serve warm.

Beef and Rutabaga Stew

Localize it

Any cut of meat will work here. You can also try using wild game such as elk or venison steaks. Try substituting the rutabaga with a turnip, kohlrabi, or a few small potatoes.

Folks often ask us what to do with rutabaga if they receive it in their CSA boxes or when they see it on display at our farmers' market stand. I always tell them to treat it like they would a potato but to know that it will offer up much more flavor. Slightly sweet and really creamy, the rutabaga is a wonderful addition to this hearty stew.

2 tablespoons cooking fat (page xv)
1 pound sirloin or strip steak, trimmed and cut into 1-inch cubes
Salt
Freshly ground black pepper
1 pound rutabaga, cut into ½-inch cubes (only peel it if the skin is super rough)
2 medium carrots, cut into ½-inch cubes
1 medium yellow onion, chopped
3 cloves of garlic, chopped
2 tablespoons tomato paste (page 39)

1 teaspoon paprika
¾ teaspoon ground cinnamon
½ teaspoon ground turmeric
½ teaspoon ground coriander
⅛ teaspoon crushed red pepper flakes (page 42)
2 tablespoons all-purpose flour
½ cup red wine
3 cups homemade or low-sodium beef broth (page 30)
Chopped parsley for serving

In a large Dutch oven or saucepan over medium, heat 1 tablespoon of the cooking fat. Sprinkle the steak with the salt and pepper and add it to the pan. Cook, stirring frequently, until the meat is no longer pink on the outside, about 4 minutes. Transfer the steak to a plate.

Add the remaining 1 tablespoon cooking fat, then the rutabaga, carrots, onion, garlic, tomato paste, paprika, cinnamon, turmeric, coriander, crushed red pepper flakes, and a pinch of salt. Cook, stirring occasionally, until the onion begins to soften and the mixture is fragrant, about 5 minutes. Add the flour and cook, stirring, for 1 minute more. Add the red wine and continue to cook, stirring to break up any bits that have stuck to the bottom of the pan. Add the broth, increase the heat to medium-high, and bring the mixture to a boil. Cook, stirring occasionally, until the rutabaga and carrots are tender, 10 to 12 minutes.

Add the steak and any accumulated juices to the pan. Reduce the heat to medium and cook the steak through, about 2 minutes longer.

Divide the stew among bowls and top it with plenty of chopped parsley. Serve with crusty bread and red wine for a complete meal.

Farmer's Pot Roast

Localize it

Any root vegetables will work here—beets, sweet potatoes, rutabagas, turnips, or celery root.

What I love about a simple pot roast is that you can usually pick up all the ingredients at your local farmers' market. It's a meal that most of the community has contributed to. Our pot roast features meat from our ranching friends Tim and Keely Jefferies, vegetables from our farm and neighboring farms, and wine from a local winemaker. When Taylor and I sit down to this humble meal, we feel the company of the familiar faces and voices of everyone who has contributed to our dinner.

2 tablespoons cooking fat (page xv)
1 (3-pound) bone-in chuck roast, trimmed
1 teaspoon salt
¼ teaspoon freshly ground black pepper
2 large onions, chopped
2 teaspoons dried thyme
1 cup dry red wine (like a Cabernet or Pinot Noir)

6 cloves of garlic, chopped
2 cups beef broth (page 30)
2 bay leaves
2 large carrots, cut into 1-inch pieces
2 parsnips, cut into 1-inch pieces (no need to peel)
2 pounds potatoes, cut into 2-inch pieces

Preheat the oven to 350°F.

In a large Dutch oven or other heavy-bottom lidded pot, heat the cooking fat over medium-high heat. Sprinkle the chuck roast with the salt and pepper. Add the roast to the pot; cook for about 5 minutes, turning it to brown it on all sides. Remove the roast to a plate and set aside.

Reduce the heat to medium-low and add the onions and thyme to the pot. Sauté until they are translucent and beginning to soften, about 8 minutes.

Return the roast to the pot. Add the red wine, garlic, beef broth, and bay leaves; bring the mixture to a simmer.

Place the lid on the pot and transfer it to the oven. Cook for 1½ hours or until the roast is almost tender.

Add the carrots, parsnips, and potatoes to the pot. Cover and bake for an additional hour or until tender. Remove and discard the bay leaves. Shred the meat using two forks.

Serve the roast over the vegetables, drizzled with the cooking liquid.

Butternut Squash Chowder

Localize it

Use any type of winter squash—pumpkin, acorn, delicata. Any dried herb will work as well.

I didn't know this until recently, but chowder has a long-standing tradition of being a communal dish. It's served year-round but most often in the colder months when folks use whatever meat, vegetables, bread, biscuits, or crackers they can find. This butternut squash chowder is a great meal to serve up with neighbors and friends who can all gather at your table on a cold winter night for a little bit of nourishment and company.

4 bacon slices, cut into
  ½-inch pieces
1 yellow onion, diced
2 cloves of garlic, minced
1 teaspoon dried sage
Pinch of ground nutmeg
Salt and freshly ground
  black pepper
2 medium-sized potatoes,
  cut into ½-inch cubes
1 small to medium butternut
  squash, cut into ½-inch cubes
  (about 4 cups)

¼ cup white wine
1 bay leaf
3 cups homemade or low-sodium
  chicken broth, stock, or
  bone broth (pages 30–31)
½ cup heavy cream
Minced parsley for garnish

In a large Dutch oven over medium heat, cook the bacon, stirring often, until it is crispy, about 5 minutes. Using a slotted spoon, transfer the bacon to a paper-towel-lined plate. Set aside.

Pour all but 1 tablespoon of the fat from the pan into a mason jar to use another time, and return the pot to medium heat. Add the onion, garlic, sage, nutmeg, a hefty pinch of salt, and 1 teaspoon of pepper. Cook, stirring occasionally, just until the vegetables are soft, 5 to 6 minutes. Stir in the potatoes and squash and cook, stirring occasionally, for about 3 minutes.

Add the wine and bay leaf and bring the mixture to a boil, stirring to scrape up the browned bits, for 1 to 2 minutes. Add the broth. Reduce the heat to low and gently simmer until the potatoes and squash are tender, about 12 minutes.

Transfer a third of the mixture to a blender and puree until it is smooth. Return it to the pot and stir in the cream. Taste for seasonings and adjust as needed.

Remove the bay leaf, ladle the soup into bowls, and top it with the bacon and parsley.

Spring

Spring has taught me the hard way that seasons don't have strict boundaries; they blend into one another like watercolors. As a farmer, the most challenging part of spring is that it starts so slowly. Sometimes mid-March can actually feel hollower than the middle of winter.

Early spring is make or break at the farm. It's when our longest, wettest, most physically demanding days take place. But there's no fresh reward after our grueling work. Instead, we sit down to another dinner of pot roast, accompanied by sprouting onions and potatoes that are growing eyes. As I prepare dinner in the early spring, I use up the last of what's sustained us through the winter. I cut mold from beets and garlic cloves, thaw any meat that hasn't spoiled. These dinners fill our bellies, but they don't exactly fill our hearts.

It's at the end of these ever-longer days that I just want to scream when I see the food magazines with their pretty photos of "seasonal" spring foods like asparagus and peas on the cover. The reality is, in March the majority of farms in the United States are still blanketed in a light snow. For us, there is a bitterness to spring—we plan for it and hope for it while winter continues to claw at our backs.

Our inaugural spring meal usually consists of mushrooms cooked over an open fire on the first nonrainy day of the season. Wild or cultivated mushrooms are available in early spring, and are divine when cooked simply with dried herbs from last season or maybe some sprigs of anything green and fresh if we've got it. Mushrooms are definitely not that salad we're craving, but they come before the first of the greens for us. So they're one step closer to what the new season has in store, and damn, are they ever delicious!

In the Pacific Northwest, this is the time when morel mushrooms start popping up in wildfire-burned areas from the previous year. Taylor and I were en route to buy a water trough for our pigs last spring when we drove by a wooded area that had been burned in the fall. It was one of the first nice days in early spring, and we'd heard from a mushroom-hunting buddy that the so-called fire morels were popping. We always have pocketknives on us, and we love going for a walk in the woods, so we pulled over.

As devastating as wildfires can be, it's incredible to witness how the land regenerates itself. Wandering those woods, heads down, spotting those first few mushrooms, was the best kind of treasure hunt. You could feel the life in the forest, the calls of animals, the vibrant new plant growth. I've learned to love roaming these scorched areas while harvesting some of the best wild edibles out there. You might spend all day hunting and only find a few morels, but then they become all the more precious. You cook them intentionally, you eat them intentionally. You slow down and ration them, not out of deprivation, but out of respect.

Finally, the snow gives way to thaw, and the green plants grow. That first salad is the stuff of dreams. You can eat it by the fistful. Just having fresh greens is a great reminder that eating in season and locally really couldn't be any simpler. You don't have to doctor it up, because it doesn't get any better than fresh greens and herbs with a light vinaigrette. That first salad will wake up the part of you that's been dormant since November.

A rule of thumb: Fruits and veggies that are harvested in the same season pair well together. Nature works like that. Think of asparagus and morels in the spring; tomatoes and basil in the summer; winter squash and apples and fresh pork in the fall. In the springtime, start talking to your local farmers or your local grocers to see what's going to be coming in. Even meat and fish are seasonal. In the spring, with eating locally, I invite you to forgo all the recipes in this book. Use them as helpful guides, but seriously: toss out your list. Go to the farmers' market, see what's emerging there, and celebrate it. Your game plan should be to not have a plan.

In most of the country, you may need to bundle up when you go to those first few markets and brace for the fact that the variety of produce you're envisioning may not yet be there. We're accustomed to getting what we want when we want it, and all those magazines with the promise of a colorful harvest don't help manage our expectations. This is your chance to reprogram those default assumptions, to have patience for that watercolor of seasons. That's really what spring is—a long, slow, desperate transition as the sun climbs to its height in the sky. An opportunity to pay attention to what your home is giving you.

Early spring is also a good time to keep working your way through your

> That's really what spring is—a long, slow, desperate transition as the sun climbs to its height in the sky.

chest freezer. Let's face it, for the first few weeks of the season you'll still be referencing the fall and winter recipes in this cookbook. Also start thinking about blanching and freezing spring goods as they come in. Plan ahead for the fleeting bounty. Pickle those garlic scapes. You can dehydrate or freeze morels, and blanch and freeze leafy greens like kale and spinach.

Later, as the afternoons grow long and warm, there will be strawberries, and it's possible you'll shed a tear when you eat your first one. There is a beauty in restraint, this inability to have it all. That's the feeling of spring. Patience, desperation, and joy, all rolled into the promise that the sun will deliver bounty in delicious phases for the next six months or more. Once the snow melts, the temperatures rise, and the first green shoots emerge from the ground, the recipes that follow will be pure delights. The best ones of the whole year, because they ring in fresh life and welcome all the nourishing seasons to come.

Go to the farmers' market, see what's emerging there, and celebrate it. Your game plan should be to not have a plan.

Spring Herb Frittata

SERVES 6

Localize it

Eggs from any fowl will do. Use whatever fresh herbs you can find. Swap ricotta or crème fraîche for the plain full-fat yogurt.

The beauty of a frittata is that it can be served for any meal. It's so easily adaptable to what's in season that you can go wild or keep it simple with your farmers' market haul. This spring version celebrates the freshness of herbs that pair well with eggs and a dollop of yogurt. This is a light, bright meal after a long, dark winter.

1 large bunch dill
½ cup plain full-fat yogurt, at room temperature
6 large eggs
2 stalks green garlic, white and green parts only (or substitute 2 cloves of garlic, minced)
1 cup firmly packed chopped parsley
Crushed red pepper flakes (page 42)
2 tablespoons olive oil
Salt and freshly ground black pepper
2 tablespoons cooking fat (page xv)

Set an oven rack 5 inches from the heat and preheat the broiler.

From the dill, set aside ½ cup firmly packed fronds. Finely mince 1 tablespoon of the dill. Reserve any remainder for another use.

In a small bowl, stir together the yogurt and the minced dill; set aside.

In a large bowl, lightly beat the eggs; set aside.

With a sharp knife, finely chop the green garlic, parsley, and reserved ½ cup dill. Place in a small bowl and toss with the crushed red pepper flakes and the oil until evenly combined. Add this mixture to the bowl with the eggs, along with a hefty pinch of salt and black pepper. Mix to combine.

In a medium-sized cast-iron skillet over medium high, heat the cooking fat until hot. Add the egg mixture and cook the frittata, lifting the cooked eggs around the edges with a rubber spatula to let the uncooked eggs flow underneath, 2 to 3 minutes. Reduce the heat to medium and cook, giving the pan a shake now and again until the eggs are mostly set but the center is still slightly jiggly, 3 to 5 minutes more.

Place the frittata in the oven and cook until the center is set and the edges are lightly browned, 12 to 15 minutes. (Watch carefully, as you can quickly overcook the frittata.)

Remove the frittata from the oven and let it rest for at least 5 minutes.

Plate and serve with a dollop of the dill yogurt. Sprinkle with more herbs, if desired.

Chilled Beet and Yogurt Soup

SERVES 4

Localize it

Try using any variety of beets here; golden, red, or striped. If beets can't be found, a chilled carrot soup would be lovely. Any fresh herb will be nice, and if you don't have lemon juice, a little red wine vinegar is a perfect substitute.

This chilled soup is flavorful and refreshing. I love how the sweet, earthy beets pair with the tangy yogurt and fresh dill. It's a simple meal to prepare as long as you cook your beets and onion in advance. And while this soup is intended to be eaten chilled, it can be served at room temperature or even slightly warm.

2 tablespoons olive oil
 or butter
1 small yellow onion,
 finely chopped
1 pound beets, cut into
 ½-inch chunks, greens
 removed and saved for
 another use

2½ cups water
¼ cup minced fresh dill,
 plus additional for serving
1 cup plain full-fat yogurt,
 plus additional for serving
2 tablespoons lemon juice
Salt and freshly ground
 black pepper

In a deep skillet over medium, heat the olive oil. Add the onion and beets and cook, stirring occasionally, until fragrant, about 5 minutes. Add the water and bring the mixture to a boil. Reduce the heat and simmer until the beets are tender, 15 to 20 minutes. Remove the skillet from the heat and let the mixture cool for about 10 minutes.

Add the beet and onion mixture to a high-speed blender along with the dill, yogurt, lemon juice, and salt and pepper to taste. Blend on the highest setting until the soup is completely smooth and creamy. Taste for seasonings and adjust as needed. If the soup is too thick, add a touch more water.

Place the soup in the fridge to chill for 1 hour.

Serve the soup with a dollop of yogurt and minced dill for garnish.

Bread Salad with Spring Greens

SERVES 4

Localize it

Use any vegetable and herb combination that's available at your farmers' market. Bulk it up with leftover chicken (page 211), lamb (page 191), or steak (page 223).

Who doesn't love a salad loaded with fresh greens and toasted bread crumbs? This dish, which is a fun twist on a classic summer tomato, bread, and herb salad (long before the tomatoes are ready), is hearty enough to be served as a complete meal or alongside grilled chicken or fish. It's refreshing, easy to prepare, and beautiful to boot. If you could pack all the delights of spring into one bowl, this is it.

4 large eggs
½ loaf of sourdough bread (page 44), torn into 1-inch pieces (about 2 cups)
¼ cup extra-virgin olive oil, plus additional for brushing
3 tablespoons red wine vinegar
1 clove of garlic, minced
1 teaspoon Dijon mustard
2 pounds asparagus, trimmed

1 cup fresh or frozen shelled peas
Salt and freshly ground black pepper
A few handfuls of arugula, Swiss chard, or spinach (or a mix)
¼ cup chopped dill
¼ cup chopped parsley
½ small red onion, thinly sliced
½ cup feta cheese, crumbled
2 to 3 radishes, thinly sliced

Preheat the oven to 350°F. Prepare a bowl of ice water and set it nearby.

Bring a large pot of water to a boil. Using a slotted spoon, gently lower the eggs into the water. Cook for 6½ to 7 minutes, maintaining a gentle boil. Remove the eggs from the water and place them in the ice water until they are cool enough to handle. Peel and slice the eggs.

Spread the bread pieces on a baking sheet and brush them lightly with olive oil. Bake for about 12 minutes or until they are crisp, shaking the pan at least once.

In a small bowl, whisk together the red wine vinegar, garlic, mustard, and ¼ cup olive oil. Season with salt and pepper.

In a large pot of boiling salted water, cook the asparagus until it is just tender, about 3 minutes. Drain, cool, and cut the asparagus in half lengthwise, noting that if some spears are really thin, they can be left whole. To the same pot add the peas; cook them for 1 to 2 minutes or until they are tender and bright green.

In a large bowl, toss the asparagus, peas, toasted bread, greens, herbs, onion, and cheese. Drizzle the dressing over the salad and toss.

Plate and serve the salad with the sliced eggs and radishes.

Green Eggs and Ham

SERVES 4

Localize it

Use bacon or sausage instead of ham, an onion instead of leeks and spinach, Swiss chard, collard greens, or bok choy leaves instead of kale. If you haven't got the chimichurri sauce on hand, you can garnish the finished dish with a drizzle of olive oil and sprinklings of crushed red pepper flakes and minced parsley.

This farm-fresh recipe is a surefire way to add some fun to your family's morning with zero food coloring necessary—and it's a great way to get little ones to eat vegetables. Even Sam-I-am would have loved this tasty, nutritious dish that can just as easily be served for a quick lunch or "breakfast as dinner."

1 tablespoon cooking fat
  (page xv)
2 medium-sized leeks, washed,
  trimmed, and thinly sliced
  (white and pale green parts only)
½ cup diced ham, bacon, or sausage
2 cloves of garlic, minced
1 teaspoon crushed red
  pepper flakes (page 42)

Salt and freshly ground black pepper
1 bunch of kale, tough stems removed,
  roughly chopped (about 5 cups)
3 to 4 eggs
Chimichurri sauce (page 33)

Preheat the oven to 350°F.

In a large cast-iron pan over medium-high heat, heat the cooking fat. Add the leeks to the pan and cook for 2 to 3 minutes, until translucent. Lower the heat to medium and continue to cook until the leeks are soft, fragrant, and beginning to brown, about 8 minutes. Add the ham, bacon, or sausage and cook through, about 5 minutes. Add the garlic, red pepper flakes, salt, and black pepper and cook for about 1 minute or until the spices are fragrant. Add the kale to the pan, in batches if needed, and let it wilt.

Take the pan off the heat and make 3 or 4 wells in the kale. Crack the eggs into the wells and place the pan in the oven for 5 to 7 minutes or until the whites are just set.

Serve with the chimichurri sauce. Enjoy!

Blistered Sugar Snap Peas with Roasted Garlic Aioli

SERVES 4 TO 6
AS A SIDE

Localize it

Instead of sugar snaps, you can blister snow peas—or even shishito peppers for a fun twist. Instead of light olive oil, you can use vegetable oil or another natural oil.

I could eat a whole bowl of these lightly charred sugar snap peas with tangy aioli all by myself. And while I know some people may consider it a sin to cook in-season sugar snap peas (they're so darn good fresh!), I think you'll be pleasantly surprised by how delicious they are when cooked in a cast-iron skillet. And bonus, the roasted garlic aioli is a great condiment to keep on hand all year long. I enjoy spreading it onto grilled burgers or using it as a dipping sauce for roasted potato wedges, grilled veggies, or even dolloped onto a nice fillet of fish. You can prepare the aioli a day or two in advance for an even quicker assembly.

FOR THE ROASTED GARLIC AIOLI
1 head of garlic
1 tablespoon olive oil or melted butter
2 egg yolks
1½ tablespoons red wine vinegar
1 teaspoon Dijon mustard
Salt
¾ cup light olive oil

FOR THE SUGAR SNAP PEAS
2 tablespoons cooking fat (page xv)
1½ pounds sugar snap peas
Flaky sea salt

Make the aioli: Preheat the oven to 425°F. Slice about ¼ inch off the top of the garlic head, exposing the tips of the individual cloves. Use your fingers to remove most of the papery outer layers of garlic skin. Drizzle the top of the garlic head with olive oil or melted butter and wrap it in aluminum foil. Place the garlic on a baking sheet and roast until it is golden brown and tender, 45 minutes to 1 hour. Remove it from the oven and when it is cool enough to handle, squeeze out the individual cloves and mash them into a paste. Set aside.

In a food processor, pulse the egg yolks, vinegar, mustard, roasted garlic paste, and a hefty pinch of salt until combined. With the machine running, slowly drizzle in the olive oil a little bit at a time until the mixture is emulsified. Taste for seasonings and adjust as needed. Transfer the aioli to a bowl and set it aside. (Extra sauce can be refrigerated in an airtight container for up to 3 days.)

Make the peas: Heat the cooking fat in a large cast-iron skillet over medium-high. Once it is hot, add the sugar snap peas (being careful as you pour them in, as the oil may splatter up a bit). Cook, stirring occasionally, until they are lightly charred and blistered on all sides, 3 to 5 minutes total.

Remove the peas from the heat and place them on a platter or bowl for serving. Sprinkle them with flaky sea salt and serve the roasted garlic aioli on the side.

Strawberries and Thyme Shortcake Biscuits

MAKES 6 SERVINGS

Localize it
Any ripe in-season berry will do.

I loved strawberry shortcake as a kiddo. And this recipe is a great reminder that you can still enjoy those old familiar flavors in a new and interesting way. With the addition of fresh thyme and sweet honey, this springtime treat is a great one to whip up when the first ripe berries of the season are ready for picking.

2 pints strawberries, sliced in half or quartered
Leaves from 4 or 5 sprigs of thyme
¼ cup honey simple syrup (page 40)

2 teaspoons apple cider vinegar
1 cup heavy cream
6 buttermilk biscuits (page 65)

Place half the berries in a bowl and gently crush them with a fork to release some of their juices. Add the remaining berries, the thyme, and 2 tablespoons of the honey simple syrup, and mix together. Drizzle in the apple cider vinegar and toss to coat. Cover the bowl with a dish towel and let the strawberries marinate for about 30 minutes.

Place a bowl and the beaters for your handheld or standing mixer in the freezer for about 15 minutes to chill. Attach the beaters to the mixer, pour the cream and remaining 2 tablespoons honey simple syrup into the bowl, and beat on low speed until the mixture is well blended. Increase the speed to high and continue to beat until peaks form and the mixture becomes thick, about 2 minutes. Place the whipped cream in the fridge until ready to use.

Slice the biscuits in half, divide the strawberries and cream among them, and serve.

Creamed Swiss Chard

SERVES 6
AS A SIDE

Localize it

Swap chard for any leafy green (spinach, kale, bok choy leaves, turnip greens, beet greens, collards).

I grew up eating my grandmother's creamed spinach. It was always a hit around the holidays, and I'd scoop big spoonfuls of the creamy dip onto slices of toasted bread. I know she used frozen spinach from the store for her classic version (which in my memory was absolutely divine); however, this version uses fresh Swiss chard from the farm and local milk, with plenty of garlic to cut through the richness of all the dairy.

Is it the lightest recipe in this book? No. But made with in-season, local ingredients, it offers plenty of nourishment and makes for a decadent side for special occasions.

1 large bunch Swiss chard
  (1 to 1¼ pounds)
¼ cup unsalted butter
¼ cup all-purpose flour
1 onion, finely chopped
3 cloves of garlic, minced
1 to 1¼ cups whole milk

Salt and freshly ground
  black pepper
Pinch of freshly grated nutmeg
Pinch of crushed red pepper flakes
  (page 42)
2 tablespoons grated hard cheese

Trim the tough inner ribs from the Swiss chard leaves and save them for another use (see Quick Pickled Chard Stems, page 258). Roughly chop the leaves.

Bring a medium-sized pot with 1 inch of salted water to a boil, and cook the chard in two batches, stirring constantly, until wilted, 1 to 2 minutes. Drain the leaves in a colander and rinse under cold running water until cool. Squeeze the chard a small handful at a time to remove as much moisture as possible.

In a medium-sized pot over medium heat, melt the butter. Whisk in the flour and cook for a couple of minutes until light golden. Add the onion and cook until it is translucent, 2 to 3 minutes, then add the garlic and cook until fragrant, about 30 seconds.

Pour in 1 cup of the milk, whisking constantly, and cook until the mixture thickens into a sauce, about 5 minutes. Season with salt, pepper, the nutmeg, and the crushed red pepper flakes. If the sauce is too thick, add the remaining ¼ cup of milk, whisking it until you reach the desired thickness.

Add the wilted chard, stirring gently to combine.

Sprinkle with the cheese and serve immediately.

Honey and Hazelnut Granola

MAKES 7 CUPS

Localize it

Swap the hazelnuts for any local nut or seed you can find. Another nut oil, like grapeseed or sunflower, or a mild-flavored oil, like light olive oil, will also work well in place of the hazelnut oil.

I grew up eating many bowls of Honey Nut Cheerios. I loved the sweet, nutty crunch of those little O's, and sipping the milk out of the bowl once the cereal was gone was my favorite part! My grown-up, local twist on that cereal includes a secret ingredient that I learned from a dear friend who is very serious about home-made granola: a single, well-beaten egg white. It binds the oats together to create a crunchier, chunkier granola. Trust me, once you try this method, you'll never go back to making granola any other way!

4 cups rolled oats
1 cup hazelnuts, coarsely chopped
2 teaspoons ground cinnamon
¼ teaspoon freshly grated nutmeg
1 teaspoon salt

¼ cup hazelnut oil
½ cup honey
2 teaspoons vanilla extract
1 large egg white, at room
   temperature

Preheat the oven to 300°F.

Combine the oats, hazelnuts, cinnamon, nutmeg, and salt in a large bowl.

Add the oil, honey, and vanilla; toss to coat. Whisk the egg white in a small bowl until it is frothy. Add it to the oat mixture and toss to coat.

Use a spatula to spread the mixture into an even layer on a rimmed baking sheet. Bake it for 20 minutes, then remove the pan from the oven and use the spatula to flip sections of the granola. Press it back into an even layer, rotate the pan, and bake for another 20 minutes. When the granola is golden and feels dry to the touch, turn off the oven and leave the pan in there for another 10 minutes to continue drying. Remove the granola from the oven and set it aside to cool completely (the granola crisps as it cools).

When it is completely cool, break the granola into clusters. Store it in an airtight container at room temperature for up to two weeks.

Pickled Garlic Scapes

MAKES 2 PINTS

Localize it

Use scallions or leeks in place of scapes.

Because the season for garlic scapes is so short, pickling is a great way to preserve the bounty for the rest of the year. Serve pickled scapes as a tangy element on a charcuterie board, tuck them inside a grilled cheese sandwich (page 118), or add them to cocktails (think Bloody Mary or martini) for a tasty garnish. They also make a beautiful hostess gift.

2 bunches garlic scapes, washed and trimmed of any woody stems
1 teaspoon black peppercorns
1 teaspoon mustard seeds
½ teaspoon crushed red pepper flakes (page 42)
½ teaspoon whole coriander seeds
1½ cups apple cider vinegar
2 tablespoons salt
2 tablespoons honey
1½ cups water

Coil each garlic scape and insert the coils into two sterilized pint-sized mason or ball jars. If your scapes are a bit older and standing more upright, you can trim them and place them upright in the jars. Fill the jars, leaving ¼ inch headspace. When the jars are full of scapes, add ½ teaspoon each of the peppercorns and mustard seeds and ¼ teaspoon of the red pepper flakes and coriander to each jar. Set them aside.

In a large pot over high heat, combine the apple cider vinegar, salt, and honey with the water. Bring the mixture to a boil, stirring until the salt and honey are dissolved. Carefully pour the boiling brine over the garlic scapes. Use a sterilized butter knife to push the garlic scapes below the rim of the jars. Wipe the rims of the jars, then twist the lids tightly into place. Let the jars come to room temperature before storing them in the refrigerator.

The scapes will keep, refrigerated, for eight to twelve months.

Braised Leeks with Walnut Bacon Crumble

SERVES 4
AS A SIDE

Localize it

If you can't get your hands on leeks, use green garlic stalks, onions, shallots, or scallions.

Leeks are one of my favorite ingredients to jazz up soups and sautés, and boost the flavor of meat dishes, but here they finally get a place at the center of our plates. Braising them really brings out the flavor, and the walnut bacon topping takes them to another level of deliciousness!

4 slices thick-cut bacon, finely chopped
8 small leeks, washed, trimmed, and halved lengthwise
2 tablespoons reserved bacon fat
Salt and freshly ground black pepper
Pinch of crushed red pepper flakes (page 42)

½ cup chicken stock, broth, or bone broth (pages 30–31)
½ cup dry white wine
½ cup walnuts, toasted and roughly chopped
¼ cup freshly grated hard cheese
2 tablespoons minced parsley

Remove any tough outer leaves from the leeks.

In a large skillet over medium heat, cook the bacon, stirring often, until cooked through and lightly crisp. With a slotted spoon, remove the bacon to a paper-towel-lined plate and set aside to drain. Pour out all but 2 table-spoons of the cooking fat into a glass jar and reserve for a later use. In the same skillet, heat the reserved bacon fat over medium-high heat. Arrange the leeks cut side down in the pan in a single layer. Cook until the cut sides are softened and golden brown, 3 to 4 minutes. Flip the leeks and continue to cook until they are softened and golden on the underside, about 3 minutes longer. If the pan is a bit dry, add another tablespoon of the reserved bacon fat or a touch of oil. Season with salt and black pepper and sprinkle with a touch of red pepper flakes. Flip the leeks again so they are cut side down. Add the stock and wine, stirring to deglaze the pan. Increase the heat to high to bring the liquid to a boil, then reduce it to a simmer, partially cover the pan, and cook until the leeks are tender and most of the liquid has evaporated.

Combine the walnuts, reserved bacon, cheese, parsley, and a pinch each of salt and black pepper in a small bowl and toss well.

Sprinkle the topping over the leeks and serve.

Lamb Kebabs with Herbed Yogurt

One of the best ways to celebrate the first warm day of spring is to fire up the grill. These lamb kebabs are a breeze to prepare and packed with so much flavor, yet take minimal effort and few ingredients. The herbed yogurt is swoonworthy—I recommend doubling the recipe so you can have leftovers in the fridge all week long for your vegetable dipping needs.

MAKES 8 SKEWERS AND
1 CUP YOGURT SAUCE

Localize it

Use beef, or even chicken, instead of lamb. For the herbed yogurt sauce, try swapping fresh mint for the dill, which will pair nicely with this lamb. Swap lemon juice for the vinegar.

FOR THE LAMB KEBABS
2 tablespoons red wine vinegar
¼ teaspoon dried thyme
¼ teaspoon dried rosemary
¼ teaspoon dried oregano
¼ teaspoon crushed red pepper flakes (page 42)
Salt
Freshly ground black pepper
¼ cup olive oil
1¼ pounds boneless lamb shoulder, cut into 1½-inch cubes
8 (8-inch) wooden skewers

FOR THE YOGURT SAUCE
¼ cup finely chopped parsley (leaves and stems are fine)
2 tablespoons minced fresh dill (fronds and stems are fine)
Hefty pinch of salt and freshly ground black pepper
2 teaspoons red wine vinegar
1 tablespoon olive oil
1 clove of garlic, minced
1 cup plain full-fat yogurt

Make the kebabs: In a large bowl, whisk together the vinegar, thyme, rosemary, oregano, red pepper flakes, and a hefty pinch of salt and freshly ground black pepper. Whisk in the oil. Add the lamb and stir the mixture to coat the lamb well with the marinade. Cover and refrigerate for at least 1 hour or even overnight.

Begin soaking the wooden skewers in water about 15 minutes before you are ready to make the kebabs. Heat an outdoor grill or grill pan to medium-high.

Remove the lamb from the marinade and thread it onto the soaked skewers.

Grill the kebabs, turning them every 2 minutes, until the lamb is cooked to the desired doneness, 6 to 8 minutes for medium-rare.

Make the yogurt sauce: Whisk everything together. Taste for seasonings and adjust.

Serve the kebabs with a side of yogurt sauce for dipping.

Spring Minestrone Soup with Pork Meatballs

SERVES 4

Localize it

Use ground chicken instead of pork. Swap chard, kale, bok choy, or collard greens for the spinach. Swap overwintered parsnips and potatoes for carrots and turnips.

This is a great soup to prepare on a spring evening when there's still a kiss of chill in the air. The ingredients are economical, easy to find locally, and the leftovers taste even better the next day. Serve with a slice of fresh sourdough bread (page 44) and a good dinner date.

1 pound ground pork
½ cup fresh bread crumbs (page 47)
3 tablespoons finely grated hard cheese, plus more for garnish
½ teaspoon dried thyme
4 cloves of garlic, chopped
1 large egg, whisked to blend
Salt and freshly ground black pepper
2 tablespoons cooking fat (page xv)
2 leeks, washed, trimmed, and sliced into ¼-inch rounds (white and pale green parts only)
Small pinch of crushed red pepper flakes (page 42)
5 cups chicken bone broth or stock (pages 30–31)
2 cups water
2 carrots, chopped (about 1 cup)
2–3 small turnips with their greens, turnips chopped (about 1 cup) and greens roughly chopped and set aside
Chopped fresh parsley for serving

In a medium bowl, mix the pork, bread crumbs, cheese, dried thyme, half the garlic, the egg, and a hefty pinch each of salt and black pepper. Form the mixture into ½-inch-diameter meatballs (you'll get about 25).

In a large pot over medium, heat the cooking fat. Cook the meatballs until they are golden all over, 3 to 4 minutes (they will finish cooking in the soup). Transfer them to a plate.

Add the leeks to the pot with a pinch of salt, pepper, and the crushed red pepper flakes and cook, stirring often, until they begin to soften, about 3 minutes. Add the remaining garlic cloves; cook for 1 minute. Add the broth and water; bring the mixture to a boil. Stir in the carrots and turnips and simmer for about 10 minutes. Add the meatballs; simmer until the vegetables are tender and the meatballs are cooked through, about 3 minutes. Add the turnip greens and continue to cook until wilted and bright green. Season with salt and pepper.

Ladle the soup into bowls. Garnish it with chopped parsley and freshly grated cheese.

Asparagus Bundles Wrapped in Bacon with Hot Honey and Sea Salt

SERVES 4 AS
AN APPETIZER

Localize it
Use prosciutto instead of bacon.

In my opinion, there's no better way to eat a spear (or two) of asparagus than when they are bear-hugged by crisp bacon and drizzled with a sweet and spicy hot honey sauce. The sauce is addictive and lasts for a long time in the fridge—I think you'll be pleased to have it on hand to drizzle over buttermilk biscuits (page 65), corn bread (page 271), or even vanilla ice cream. A sprinkle of flaky sea salt ties it all together with a satisfying bit of crunch.

FOR THE HOT HONEY
3 hot chile peppers
   (such as cayenne, Fresno,
   or Thai)
1 cup honey

18 asparagus stalks
6 slices of thick-cut bacon
1 tablespoon olive oil
Flaky sea salt

Make the hot honey: Thinly slice the peppers, scraping out the seeds from one whole pepper and reserving them; you'll want to save these seeds to add later if the honey isn't quite spicy enough.

In a small saucepan, bring the honey and peppers to a bare simmer over medium-low heat. Reduce the heat to low and cook for about 45 minutes, stirring the honey every 10 minutes or so. Taste the honey and adjust the heat by adding the reserved seeds if it's not spicy enough. Let the mixture cool for 30 minutes before straining and transferring it to a sealed jar. If some of the seeds don't strain (or you wish to leave some in for added kick), that's just fine, the honey will become a bit spicier over time, but we like that! The honey will last for three months in an airtight container in the refrigerator.

Make the asparagus: Preheat the oven to 425°F. Wrap 3 asparagus stalks at a time with a slice of bacon. Place the bundle on a rimmed baking sheet and repeat until all the stalks have been wrapped with bacon slices.

Drizzle the olive oil over the asparagus bundles. Toss lightly to coat. Place the asparagus in the oven and bake until the asparagus is cooked through and the bacon is done, about 15 minutes.

Drizzle the asparagus bundles with the hot honey, sprinkle them with sea salt, and serve.

Tuna Steaks with Green Sauce

SERVES 2

Note

This recipe also tastes great served cold. So save leftovers in Tupperware and serve chilled for lunch or a snack.

Localize it

Any white-fleshed fish will work here.

I'll never look at a tuna the same way after my experience on a boat off the Oregon coast. Between the treacherous waters and reeling in fish a quarter of my weight, my arms are still sore! But good-quality tuna from a reputable source makes all the difference. If you're lucky enough to live on or near the coast, this recipe is for you. For everyone else, use this as a blueprint to prepare any white fish with the green sauce, knowing that the end result will be quite different, but equally delicious.

1 albacore tuna loin, 1½ pounds
1–2 tablespoons nut, seed, or olive oil

Chimichurri sauce (page 33)

Heat a large cast-iron pan (in which the loin will fit) over medium-high heat. Add the oil and allow it to heat.

Place the loin in the pan and sear it on each side for approximately 1 minute. Albacore is very lean, so it's best not to cook it all the way through. You can look at the cut end of the loin to gauge how deeply the tuna has cooked. If you're using another type of white fish, adjust the cooking time to a bit longer so it cooks completely through. This will add just a few more minutes to your total cooking time.

Remove the tuna from the pan and let it rest, tented with foil, for about 5 minutes.

Cut the loin crosswise into ½-inch-thick slices, lightly sawing through the fish so you do not tear it.

Serve with chimichurri sauce.

Steak with Radish and Pea Shoot Salad and Yogurt

SERVES 4

Localize it

Use lamb chops, venison, or elk in place of beef steak. For the salad, try thinly sliced salad turnips instead of radishes or shaved asparagus instead of the pea shoots.

This is a simple weeknight recipe that is hearty and satisfying. When you take a forkful of the steak with a bit of crunchy salad dressed with creamy, slightly tart yogurt, each bite feels like a celebration of the best parts of spring.

2 (1-pound) New York strip or
   sirloin steaks (about 1¼ inch thick)
Salt and freshly ground
   black pepper
1 tablespoon cooking fat
   (page xv)

3 tablespoons olive oil
1 tablespoon red wine vinegar
4 radishes, trimmed and thinly sliced
1 cup fresh pea shoots
1 cup plain full-fat yogurt

Pat the steaks dry with paper towels. Season them with plenty of salt and pepper.

In a cast-iron skillet over medium-high, heat the cooking fat.

Add the steaks and cook to the desired doneness, 5 to 6 minutes per side for medium-rare. Let them rest for 10 minutes.

In a small bowl, whisk together the olive oil, vinegar, and a pinch of salt and pepper.

In a large bowl, combine the radishes and pea shoots with the vinaigrette.

Spread a thin layer of yogurt onto each serving plate. Sprinkle with salt and pepper. Slice the steak and place it over the yogurt; top with the salad.

Spring Pea and Salmon Chowder

SERVES 4

Localize it

Salmon can be swapped for any local fish: cod, halibut, or trout. Spring onions will work instead of leeks, and turnips can be replaced with young potatoes or kohlrabies. Any mix of fresh spring herbs will be divine.

If you could forage all the fresh flavors of spring and put them together in the same bowl, this would be the recipe of the season. Sweet peas, young turnips, zesty herbs, fresh-caught salmon, and a light, just-creamy-enough base—this is the kind of chowder I could eat all season long.

3 leeks, washed and trimmed (white and pale green parts only)
1 pound Japanese turnips
2 tablespoons cooking fat (page xv)
2 cloves of garlic, minced
2 teaspoons salt
Freshly ground black pepper
Pinch of crushed red pepper flakes (page 42)
1 cup chicken stock (page 31)

2 bay leaves
2 cups water
1 pound salmon fillet, skin discarded, cut into 1-inch pieces
1 cup heavy cream
10 ounces fresh shelled sweet peas or thawed frozen sweet peas
1 tablespoon fresh lemon juice
¼ cup finely chopped dill
¼ cup finely chopped parsley
Flaky sea salt

Slice the leeks into ¼-inch rounds. Use your fingers to separate them into individual rings. (It's okay if some stick together, though.) Remove the greens from the turnips and save them for another use. Slice the turnips in half or in quarters if they're larger than 1½ inches in diameter.

Warm the cooking fat in a large Dutch oven or soup pot over medium heat. Add the leeks and cook, stirring occasionally, until the leeks begin to soften, 5 to 6 minutes. Add the garlic, turnips, 1 teaspoon of the salt, a hefty pinch of black pepper, and the red pepper flakes. Stir to combine. Add the stock, bay leaves, and water and bring the mixture to a boil. Reduce the heat to medium-low and cook, uncovered, until the turnips are fork-tender, 8 to 10 minutes.

Season the salmon with the remaining 1 teaspoon salt. Add it to the pot along with the cream and peas. Cook, stirring occasionally, until the salmon is cooked through and breaks apart a bit as you stir, 5 to 8 minutes. Remove the chowder from the heat and stir in the lemon juice and herbs.

Ladle the chowder into bowls and season it with flaky sea salt and more black pepper.

Butter Beans with Green Sauce

SERVES 4 TO 6
AS A SIDE

Note

If you prepare your beans in advance, they'll stay fresh in a sealed container in the fridge for up to 5 days.

Localize it

Use any white bean instead of butter beans, or swap out the chimichurri for sun-dried tomato pesto or olive tapenade.

I love this side dish for many reasons. First, it's simple to prepare, especially if you precook your beans ahead of time. Second, it's really light and refreshing, and pairs well with a variety of main courses. Try serving these beans alongside grilled chicken thighs, poached salmon, or spooned over toasted sourdough bread (page 44).

¾ pounds dried butter beans
4 cloves of garlic, 2 left whole, 2 thinly sliced
1 bay leaf
Salt
2 tablespoons cooking fat (page xv)
¼ teaspoon crushed red pepper flakes (page 42)

¼ cup dry white wine
Flakey sea salt and freshly ground black pepper
½ cup chicken stock, vegetable stock, or water (page 31)
Chimichurri sauce (page 33)
Flaky sea salt for serving

Prepare the butter beans by rinsing them in a colander under cool water. Pick out any debris or shriveled beans. Place them in a bowl with enough water to cover them by at least 3 inches. Soak for 6 to 8 hours (adding more water if needed). Drain and rinse the beans and place them in a large pot along with 2 whole garlic cloves, 1 bay leaf, and a pinch of salt. Cover them with 3 inches of water and bring to a boil. Immediately reduce the heat to low. Cover the pot and keep over low heat until the beans are cooked through, adding more water as needed, about 1 hour (times will vary, depending on the freshness of your dried beans). Drain the beans and discard the garlic and bay leaf.

In a 10-inch skillet, heat the cooking fat over medium-low. Add the sliced garlic and red pepper flakes and cook until fragrant, about 1 minute. Pour in the wine and bring to a boil. Immediately reduce the heat to medium-low, add the beans to the skillet, and season with salt and pepper. Cook, stirring occasionally, until the flavors have blended, 2 to 3 minutes. Use a wooden spoon to smash about one third to one half of the beans (this adds a nice texture).

Add the stock or water and bring the mixture to a simmer. Cook 1 to 2 minutes more or until the sauce becomes creamy and is reduced by about half.

Transfer the beans to a bowl and stir in a few tablespoons of chimichurri. Season with flaky salt.

Roasted Radishes with Anchovies

Our farmers' market customers and CSA members receive a lot of radishes for six months out of the year. And while I love to eat radishes straight up like an apple, roasting them mellows the flavor a bit. The addition of salty, umami anchovies sends the wow factor of this simple side dish off the charts. We eat these radishes like popcorn!

1 large or 2 small bunches of radishes (about 13 radishes total), sliced in half (smaller ones can be left whole)

6 anchovy fillets, finely chopped

2 cloves of garlic, finely chopped

2 to 3 tablespoons olive oil

Pinch each of salt and freshly ground black pepper

1 to 2 teaspoons red wine vinegar for serving

Localize it

Use salad turnips instead of radishes. Chop up a few olives and capers instead of anchovies to make this vegetarian. The flavor and texture will be different, but you'll still get that salty accent.

Preheat the oven to 375°F.

In a large bowl, toss the radishes with the anchovy fillets, garlic, oil, salt, and pepper.

Place the coated radishes on a baking sheet and roast them until they are deeply browned and shriveled a bit, 30 to 35 minutes. Toss them halfway through the cooking time.

Remove the baking sheet from the oven and drizzle the radishes with the red wine vinegar.

Serve the radishes as a side dish alongside a main course or eat them straight off the baking sheet for a quick snack!

Grilled Garlic Scapes

SERVES 4 TO 6
AS A SIDE

Localize it

Use leeks or scallions
instead of garlic scapes.

This recipe is a great way to highlight a seasonal favorite. Grilling the scapes adds a charred flavor and helps mellow their aggressive bite. You can use this method for grilling any allium veggies (scallions, leeks, onions, whole garlic cloves) to make them a main event instead of just an accent.

2 bunches of garlic scapes
2 tablespoons melted or liquid
  cooking fat (page xv)

Flaky sea salt

Preheat an outdoor grill to medium.

In a medium bowl, toss the scapes with the cooking fat until evenly coated.

Place the scapes in a single layer on the grill (you may need to do this in batches) and grill until they are lightly charred on both sides, 2 to 3 minutes per side.

Plate and serve them sprinkled with flaky sea salt.

Egg Salad with Fresh Herbs on Toast

SERVES 4

Localize it

You can use duck, quail, or goose eggs instead of chicken eggs. Use any fresh herbs you can find.

Eating locally doesn't get more basic and delicious than this toasted bread with egg salad. This is one of those humble, local meals that you can make anywhere—you can get fresh eggs, bread, and herbs for much of the year no matter where you live. Serve it with a side of bacon at breakfast or tossed greens for lunch and dinner.

8 large eggs
½ cup mayonnaise (page 33)
2 scallions, very thinly sliced
1 clove of garlic, minced
Salt and freshly ground
   black pepper
¼ cup torn basil leaves
¼ cup chopped dill
   (fronds and stems)
¼ cup chopped parsley
   (leaves and stems)

Pinch of crushed red pepper flakes
   (page 42)
1 teaspoon red wine vinegar
Olive oil for drizzling
Flaky sea salt
4 teaspoons Dijon mustard
4 slices sourdough bread
   (page 44), toasted

Bring a large saucepan filled with salted water to a boil over high heat. Prepare a bowl filled with ice water and set it nearby.

Reduce the heat to maintain an active simmer and gently lower the eggs into the water; cook them for 8½ minutes. Immediately transfer the eggs with a slotted spoon to the ice water.

When the eggs are cool enough to handle, pat them dry and peel them. Chop the eggs into large pieces and add them to a medium-sized bowl, along with the mayo, scallions, and garlic. Gently toss the eggs to coat in the mayo mixture. Season with salt and black pepper to taste. Set aside.

In a small bowl, toss the basil, dill, parsley, and red pepper flakes. Add the red wine vinegar, drizzle the mixture with oil, and season with flaky sea salt. Toss to coat.

Spread 1 teaspoon of the mustard onto each slice of toasted bread. Spoon the eggs over the bread. Pile the herb mixture on top of the egg toast and serve.

Simple Roasted Chicken

Note

You can use this same method for a larger bird, but the cooking time will be longer.

Localize it

I wouldn't swap the method for this with any other poultry. You can swap out the butter for olive oil and use any mixture of herbs you'd like (or simply leave the herbs out).

Every home cook needs to know how to roast a chicken—and there's nothing more comforting than the smell of chicken roasting in your oven. It should be pretty easy for you to buy a whole chicken locally, and it's such an economical meal. Use leftovers for chicken salad (page 220), slice it for sandwiches during the week, and use the carcass to make stock or bone broth (page 30).

One 4- to 5-pound farm-fresh chicken
Salt and freshly ground black pepper
6 cloves of garlic

½ of a large yellow or red onion
4 to 6 sprigs fresh herbs (thyme, rosemary, oregano)
¼ cup melted butter

Preheat the oven to 425°F.

Rinse the chicken, then dry it very well with paper towels, inside and out.

Salt and pepper the cavity. Stuff the cavity with the garlic cloves, onion, and herbs, then use kitchen twine to truss the bird. Trussing isn't necessary, but it does help the bird cook more evenly.

Drizzle the melted butter all over the chicken, then generously salt the chicken (about 1 tablespoon's worth). Season to taste with pepper.

Place the chicken in a cast-iron pan or roasting pan and, when the oven is up to temperature, put the chicken in the oven. Roast it until it's done, about 1½ hours.

Baste the chicken with the pan juices and let it rest for 15 minutes before removing the chicken to a cutting board to slice and serve.

Kohlrabi and Carrot Slaw with Smoked Tuna

SERVES 4

Localize it
Swap regular tuna for smoked tuna or even leftover shredded chicken. Swap salad turnips or thinly sliced broccoli stems for the kohlrabi.

Who doesn't love a good slaw recipe that's packed with fresh, crispy vegetables and, in this case, some protein? This spring stew is hearty enough to be served as a main-course salad. I also like to pile a big scoop on top of a slice of grilled sourdough bread (page 44) slathered with a bit of mayonnaise (page 33).

2 carrots, julienned
1 kohlrabi, peeled and julienned
½ a small red onion, thinly sliced
Salt and freshly ground black pepper
⅓ cup plain full-fat yogurt
Splash of red wine vinegar
5 ounces smoked albacore tuna
Extra-virgin olive oil for drizzling
¼ cup minced parsley

In a large bowl, combine the carrots, kohlrabi, and onion and season them with a bit of salt and pepper.

In a smaller bowl, combine the yogurt, vinegar, tuna, a hefty pinch of salt, a drizzle of oil, and pepper. Mix well. Add the mixture to the bowl with the veggies and toss in the parsley. Taste for seasonings and adjust as needed before serving.

Chicken with 40 Cloves of Garlic

Localize it

Swap rabbit, quail, duck, or any game bird for the chicken. Use turnips instead of potatoes. Rosemary or oregano instead of thyme would work, or a mix of all.

This is one of those awesome spring recipes to make while it's still cool in the evenings. You'll most likely be using overwintered garlic cloves and potatoes, unless you're lucky enough to get some new potatoes in certain parts of the country. This is a crowd-pleasing dish that's simple to prepare for a weeknight and elegant enough for a dinner party. Serve it with a baguette to mop up any pan juices.

2 tablespoons cooking fat (page xv)
8 small bone-in, skin-on chicken thighs
Salt and freshly ground black pepper
40 garlic cloves, peeled
¼ cup dry white wine
¾ cup homemade or low-sodium chicken broth (page 30)
1 pound small potatoes, halved
6 fresh thyme sprigs
Small bunch of parsley, roughly chopped

Preheat the oven to 425°F.

Melt the cooking fat in a large, heavy saucepan or Dutch oven over medium-high heat. Meanwhile, season the chicken thighs on all sides with salt and pepper. Add the chicken in batches to the hot pan, skin side down, taking care to avoid crowding, and cook them for about 6 minutes or until they are golden brown; turn and repeat on the other side. Transfer each browned batch to a plate and set aside.

Add the garlic to the saucepan and cook, stirring often, until the cloves are lightly browned and beginning to soften, 2 to 3 minutes. Pour the wine into the hot saucepan and stir to scrape up the browned bits on the bottom of the pan; bring the wine to a simmer. Cook until it reduces by half, about 2 minutes. Add the broth and return the mixture to a simmer. Add the potatoes and season with salt and pepper.

Tuck the browned chicken thighs in a single layer between the potatoes. Spoon some of the cooking liquid over the chicken thighs. Scatter with the thyme springs and parsley.

Roast in the oven until the potatoes are fork-tender and the chicken is cooked through, 35 to 40 minutes.

Serve the chicken and potatoes with a drizzle of the pan juices.

Spring Vegetable Stew

SERVES 4

Localize it

Any spring vegetables will work here. Try overwintered parsnips in place of (or in addition to) carrots. Spring peas would also be a delicious addition, and leftover shredded chicken or pork would be great added to the pot as well. Have a handful of kale or Swiss chard? Chop that up and throw it in toward the end!

This spring stew is a great way to incorporate the local harvest and is the perfect meal when served with a side salad, toasted sourdough bread (page 44), and a glass of crisp white wine. Quick note: You can soak and cook the beans ahead of time to make everything come together a little faster!

1 bunch of asparagus, cut into 1-inch lengths
1 cup dried white beans (such as navy or cannellini), soaked overnight, drained
2 cloves of garlic, peeled and left whole
2 tablespoons cooking fat (page xv)
2 bunches scallions, chopped (white and pale green parts only)
¼ pound mushrooms (any combination of wild or cultivated in-season mushrooms), roughly chopped
6 small white turnips, cut into wedges

1 small kohlrabi, peeled and cut into ½-inch pieces
2 medium carrots, cut into 1-inch-long sticks
Salt and freshly ground black pepper
1 teaspoon dried thyme
½ cup dry white wine
5 to 6 cups vegetable stock (page 31)
Chimichurri sauce (page 33) for serving
Freshly grated hard salty cheese for serving
1 small bunch of parsley, finely chopped, for serving

Bring a medium pot of salted water to a simmer and add the asparagus. Cook over medium-high heat until the asparagus is tender, about 4 minutes. Using a slotted spoon, transfer it to a bowl. Add the white beans and garlic to the water, making sure they're covered by at least 2 inches, and bring it to a boil. Immediately, reduce the heat and simmer until the beans are tender, 50 minutes to 1 hour (this will depend on the freshness of your beans). Drain the beans, discard the garlic, and transfer the beans to the bowl with the asparagus. Set aside.

In a medium-sized cast-iron pot or Dutch oven, heat 1 tablespoon of the cooking fat. Add the scallions and mushrooms and cook over medium heat until tender, about 3 minutes. Heat the remaining tablespoon of cooking fat and add the turnips, kohlrabi, and carrots; season the veggies with a hefty pinch of salt and pepper and the dried thyme. Cook, stirring occasionally, for about 3 minutes longer.

Add the wine to the pan and cook, stirring up any browned bits off the bottom of the pot, until most of the liquid has evaporated. Add 5 cups of the stock to the pot and bring it to a simmer. Add in the reserved beans and asparagus. If the soup seems too thick, add an additional cup of stock to thin as needed.

Ladle the soup into individual bowls and stir a small dollop of the chimichurri into each bowl. Sprinkle with freshly grated cheese and minced parsley.

Ham, Pea, and Leek Pasta

SERVES 4

Localize it

Swap the leeks for spring onions, shallots, green garlic, or scallions for a different yet equally delicious twist. Swap the peas for green beans, and try pork sausage instead of the ham steaks.

I love cooking with fresh peas in the spring—they really are worth the wait. Here the saltiness of the ham paired with the sweet, tender peas is a match made in heaven. This is a great pasta dish to whip up on a busy weeknight: It offers plenty of nutrition, it's bursting with flavor, and it's super kid-friendly!

1 pound pasta (any type)
3 tablespoons unsalted butter
3 leeks, washed, trimmed, and thinly sliced (white and pale green parts only)
10 ounces fresh or frozen shelling peas
¼ pound ham steak, roughly chopped

½ cup dry white wine or chicken stock (page 31)
¾ cup heavy cream
4 ounces ricotta cheese
⅓ cup chopped fresh dill
Salt and freshly ground black pepper
Crushed red pepper flakes (page 42)

Bring a large pot of salted water to a boil and add the pasta. Cook until al dente. Drain and return the pasta to the pot, then toss it with 1 tablespoon of the butter to prevent sticking.

Meanwhile, in a large skillet, heat the remaining 2 tablespoons butter over medium-high heat. Add the leeks and cook until golden, about 4 minutes. Add the peas and ham and cook until the peas are hot and the ham is lightly browned, about 5 minutes. Add the wine, crank the heat up, and cook, stirring occasionally, until it's reduced by about half, about 1 minute. Stir in the cream, reduce the heat to medium, and cook, stirring often, until the sauce is slightly thickened, 3 to 5 minutes.

Pour the cream sauce into the pasta pot, add the ricotta and dill, and season with plenty of salt and black pepper. Sprinkle with red pepper flakes to taste.

Classic Chicken Salad with Kohlrabi

SERVES 4

Localize it

If you don't have chicken, try using turkey or rabbit instead. If you don't have kohlrabi, try swapping in another fresh crunchy vegetable, like celery or Swiss chard stems.

Nothing hits the spot quite like a chicken salad sandwich. It's a great way to use leftover chicken from a whole roasted chicken and makes a perfect picnic lunch to pack if you're heading out to the beach or lake, or just dining al fresco in your backyard.

2 cups diced cooked chicken
½ cup peeled and diced kohlrabi
1 small red onion, diced
½ cup mayonnaise (page 33)
2 teaspoons Dijon mustard

1 tablespoon red wine vinegar
2 tablespoons minced fresh parsley
Salt and freshly ground black pepper
Lettuce leaves or bread for serving

In a medium-sized bowl, combine the chicken, kohlrabi, onion, mayo, mustard, vinegar, and parsley. Season to taste with salt and pepper and stir again. Serve on lettuce leaves or bread.

Grilled Steak with Herb Butter

Localize it

Any cut of red meat will work. You can also try venison or elk steaks.

I love the simplicity of grilled steak on a weeknight here at the farm. It's such an easy, no-fuss kind of meal that always satisfies our hunger and leaves us feeling nourished. This steak is served with an incredibly delicious herb butter that takes a simple cut of grilled meat and turns it into something special.

4 rib-eye steaks, 1¼ inches thick
Salt and freshly ground
   black pepper

¼ cup herb butter
   (page 34)

Preheat a grill to high heat.

Place the rib-eye steaks on a large platter and season them with salt and pepper. Transfer the steaks to the hot grill and cook for 4 to 6 minutes on each side for medium-rare, longer if desired. Let the steaks rest for 5 to 10 minutes before serving.

Plate the steaks and add 1 tablespoon of herb butter to each.

Mushrooms Cooked over Fire

SERVES 4
AS A SIDE

Localize it

Sorry, folks, there's no substitute for mushrooms, but you can use any kind you like here. You can also sub white wine vinegar and white wine for the red wine vinegar and red wine. Use any fresh herbs you prefer.

This is an interactive side dish. It's a fun one to make when you're camping or in the backyard with neighbors and friends. Mushrooms slowly cooked over a flame just have a beautiful smoky flavor, and this presentation, straight out of the skillet, is rustic and fun.

¼ cup unsalted butter or other cooking fat (page xv)

1½ pounds wild or cultivated mushrooms (small mushrooms can be left whole and larger ones can be chopped to about ½-inch pieces)

2 cloves of garlic, minced

1 sprig thyme

1 tablespoon red wine vinegar

¼ cup red wine

Salt and freshly ground black pepper

In a large cast-iron skillet over an open flame (or the stovetop, if an open flame isn't possible), heat the butter.

Add the mushrooms, garlic, and thyme. Stir, and cook for 8 to 10 minutes, until the mushrooms are slightly soft and have released some of their juices. The cooking time will depend on how hot the fire is. Add the vinegar, stir, and cook for 1 minute. Add the wine and cook it down for about 5 minutes. Season with salt and pepper.

Serve the mushrooms over grilled steaks, grilled chicken, grilled bread, or as is.

Pork Loin with Kohlrabi Mash

SERVES 6

Tip: It's easiest to peel the kohlrabi with a sharp knife rather than a vegetable peeler, as the skin is very thick.

Localize it: This dish would taste great with a variety of different meats, such as pork chops, chicken thighs, steak, or fish. Remember, cooking times will vary if you use a different cut of meat. Try mincing garlic scapes or spring onions instead of the green garlic. For the mash, try using turnips, rutabaga, celery root, or a combination of them all! Any fresh or dried herb will work in the rub for the pork.

This is a lovely spring meal that utilizes a few of my favorite ingredients. First, I love the simplicity of a roasted pork loin. It's so darn flavorful with minimal ingredients and not a lot of fuss. Second, kohlrabi mash just may be my favorite mashed vegetable. It's got a slight sweet and nutty flavor that I absolutely adore and it's really versatile. Try it at Thanksgiving with your turkey or as a side to any grilled meat or fish dish. Mashed kohlrabi is a great recipe to keep on hand for most of the year because kohlrabi is available year-round in most places.

4 large green garlic stalks, white and pale green parts only, or 4 cloves garlic, minced
4 teaspoons chopped fresh thyme or 2 teaspoons dried thyme
Hefty pinch of salt and pepper
2½ pounds boneless pork loin, trimmed
¼ cup finely chopped parsley

FOR THE KOHLRABI MASH
2½ pounds kohlrabi (about 2 medium-sized ones), peeled and cut into large chunks (see tip)
2 tablespoons heavy cream
3 tablespoons unsalted butter
Hefty pinch of salt and pepper
Pinch of crushed red pepper flakes (page 42)

Preheat the oven to 400°F.

In a small bowl, mix together the garlic, thyme, salt, and pepper with your hands until well combined.

Place the pork loin on a rack in a roasting pan and, with your hands, massage the garlic/herb mixture all over. Turn the pork fat side down on the rack and roast in the oven for 30 minutes. Remove from the oven and turn the pork fat side up. Continue to roast for about 25 minutes longer or until a meat thermometer inserted into the center of the loin registers 155°F. Remove the loin from the oven and let it rest for 15 minutes before slicing.

Meanwhile, prepare the kohlrabi mash. Fill a medium-sized saucepan with water and add the kohlrabi. Bring to a boil, reduce the heat, and simmer until the kohlrabi is fork tender, about 20 minutes. Drain.

Add the kohlrabi, cream, butter, salt, pepper, and crushed red pepper flakes to a food processor or blender and process until smooth (it's okay if there are a few lumps). Alternately, you can use an immersion blender to achieve the same consistency. Taste for seasonings and adjust as needed.

Spread the kohlrabi mash onto a platter. Top with the sliced pork loin and season the whole dish with additional salt, pepper, and crushed red pepper flakes to taste. Sprinkle with the parsley and serve warm.

Summer

For Taylor and me, summer is go-time. The days are long, and every part of the farm is cranking at full speed, including the weeds. The weeks fly by as we get more and more fatigued. The dirt in the creases of our hands and under our fingernails becomes permanent, and our skin turns to leather under the blazing sun. Sometimes we find ourselves dreaming of the long, slow dark of winter. The bounty of fresh food from the farm is amazing, but it's also overwhelming, and I find myself feeling like a frantic squirrel during an acorn boom, trying to put everything away for winter—canning tomatoes and cherries, making batch after batch of freezer pesto and chimichurri and zucchini butter, pickling peppers. It's hard to find the time to eat, so it's a good thing ingredients are fresh, plentiful, and simple to prepare. Salads of fresh greens tossed in oil, meat and vegetables thrown on the grill . . . It's easy to prepare lovely local food in the summer.

But to really capture the feeling of eating locally during this season of plenty, I want to tell you a story.

A typical farmers' market day for us in the summer is so hustling and bustling that Taylor and I usually don't get to eat a proper meal. One Saturday this past August, I realized I was starving. After all, slinging veggies is tough work—we're up before four A.M. to pack our trailer with a couple thousand pounds of produce and our stall setup to drive the fifteen miles to the market and get everything ready before the bell rings at nine A.M. For the next four hours, the stream of customers is constant. They're stoked to see us, and we love to catch up with them, so there's a lot of talking, and because we're cash-only, there's also a lot of mental math involved. So by eleven o'clock, both Taylor and I are usually ravenous. Most of the time we come prepared with snacks, but this particular day was very, very busy and totally snackless.

I was desperate. As soon as the customer flow slowed down enough that I didn't feel like I was throwing Taylor to the wolves, I grabbed some cash and took off. We typically tag out to go pick up something from a local restaurant, but we were in the midst of our local food challenge, so I decided to stay in the market.

It took me a couple of seconds in my famished state to figure out a plan, but I said to myself, okay, our neighboring farmer is baking baguettes, so we've got bread. Vine-ripened summer tomatoes are everywhere. There's prosciutto from local pasture-raised pigs and cheese from a local dairy and creamery. I thought, *Yeah, I can work with that.* So I went and grabbed it all, whipped out my trusty pocketknife, and assembled a makeshift sandwich. In my mind I'd thought I'd need balsamic vinegar or olive oil to moisten the bread and add a little flavor, or salt and pepper to bring everything to life. But I didn't have any of that, and it turned out I didn't need it. All the seasoning in the world was in the prosciutto and in the cheese, and the juicy tomato sauced the whole thing up. A summer tomato is better than filet mignon. It can't be beat.

Honest to God, it was the best sandwich I've ever eaten in my life. And every ingredient in it came from a parking lot where all the local vendors that live in my valley had gathered. Forget two hundred miles, this was a meal created within one hundred feet.

Moral of the story: In our neck of the woods—and I believe in many parts of the country—the summer bounty makes eating simply, locally, and on a budget really easy. And in-season, quality food doesn't need dressing up.

Early August at the farmers' market is chaos. From May through October, every Saturday morning, farmers across the United States wake up extra early, overly caffeinate themselves, and haul their bounty to local markets in hopes of selling out. Their livelihoods depend on it. The way I see things, it's sort of the community's job to support these efforts. To show up. To acknowledge the fact that these folks have put in a full day by nine A.M. That they're extra tired, they're extra flustered, and oftentimes they're actually starving, despite the bounty surrounding them.

A summer tomato
is better than filet
mignon. It can't
be beat.

I encourage you to throw a cooler in the car on your way out to the market. Don't just buy treats. Buy your groceries for the week and eat like royalty. The farmers and our communities, we rely on each other; it's a give and take. As farmers, we rely on our neighbors to support us, so that we can supply them with really good-quality food. At a lot of farmers' markets, you can even get a cheap meal. All you need is a knife. So here's another suggestion: When you go to the farmers' market, don't forget your pocketknife.

For farmers, summer really is the season when being home is the most special. The days are so long that you're able to eat breakfast, lunch, and dinner out on the patio. Long days make for late dinners. I know that for many folks, summer is a time for vacations and beach trips and other activities, but there are treasures to be found right at home when you really slow down and take in the season. It's like a long, hot, meditative calm. Sometimes it can seem like summertime rolls out ahead of you forever. By August everyone's complaining about the heat and looking forward to fall. I guess what I'm getting at is this: Try not to rush through the magic of the days when you can walk barefoot, when you can sit outside in a T-shirt and eat a juicy slice of watermelon. Living in the moment happens naturally when you're eating with the seasons. You experience directly how the seasons disappear as quickly as they come. In summer, I want to enjoy every single moment, savor every single flavor.

Summer is the cheapest time of the year to eat, and you're going to eat really well. It's also probably the healthiest time to eat—you can get fruits and veggies straight off the vine and tree. Fall is when you're going to invest, when you'll buy half a cow to fill your freezer and stock up on winter squash from the last few farmers' markets of the year. Summer is a great time to save money, to buy just what your family needs to get through the week, and eat the freshest, most nutritious stuff available. Summer cooking is as easy as firing up the grill. The beauty of all the foods available is the simplicity of cooking them outside.

Remember the rule of thumb that foods that grow together and are harvested at the same time taste good together—so if you're wondering whether Swiss chard pairs well with tomatoes, yes it does. In the summertime, some of the best recipes write themselves when you just grab random ingredients that are fresh and available and prepare them simply. These recipes were created in that spirit. They're about making easy picnics and backyard barbecues. Food that's meant to be celebrated and shared.

This past year, summer reminded me that eating locally isn't about depriving yourself. I think what it's really about is cultivating awareness. Because when you're aware of exactly where your food is coming from, every bite is full of joy. You stop thinking of things as disposable; you look at what you've got, and you honor and celebrate each ingredient. In the summer, we have so much. And we don't have to go far for it. Just like when I stood in that hot parking lot on an August morning, eating like a queen and knowing each person who contributed to my incredible, five-ingredient meal. You kind of want to pinch yourself.

Try not to rush through the magic of the days when you can walk barefoot, when you can sit outside in a T-shirt and eat a juicy slice of watermelon.

Huckleberry Cornmeal Pancakes

Localize it

Any berry will be good here. If you don't have buttermilk, whole milk will work just fine here. If you're out of honey, homemade jam or maple syrup will substitute well.

I grew up eating pancakes every Sunday morning. They were something to look forward to, and I still feel like pancakes are a special treat. These cornmeal berry cakes are super simple to make and couldn't be more delicious. If you're lucky enough to live in a part of the country where maple syrup is available locally, go wild drizzling these puppies with the good stuff.

½ cup cornmeal
1½ cups all-purpose flour, plus 1 teaspoon for coating the berries
1½ teaspoons baking powder
1½ teaspoons baking soda
1¼ teaspoons salt
2½ cups buttermilk
2 large eggs
2 tablespoons honey, heated until pourable

3 tablespoons unsalted butter, melted, plus more butter for serving
1½ cups huckleberries
1 teaspoon ground cinnamon
Vegetable oil or ghee (or any high-heat oil) for the skillet
Honey simple syrup (page 40) for serving

Preheat the oven to 325°F.

In a large bowl, whisk together the cornmeal, flour, baking powder, baking soda, and salt. Make a well in the center. Pour the buttermilk into the well and crack the eggs into the buttermilk. Drizzle in the honey and pour the melted butter into the mixture. Starting in the center, whisk everything together, moving toward the outside of the bowl, until all the ingredients are incorporated. Do not overmix—lumps are fine.

Coat the berries in a teaspoon of flour (so that they don't sink) and the teaspoon cinnamon. Stir them into the batter. The batter can be refrigerated for up to 1 hour.

Heat a large, well-seasoned cast-iron skillet over low heat for about 5 minutes. Add 1 tablespoon oil. Turn the heat up to medium-low and, using a measuring cup, ladle ⅓ cup batter into the skillet, repeating with more batter to make more pancakes, taking care not to overcrowd the pan.

Flip the pancakes when bubbles rise to the surface and the bottoms begin to brown, 2 to 4 minutes. When both sides of the pancakes are lightly browned, remove them to a rimmed baking sheet and keep them in the heated oven until all the batter is cooked.

Serve the pancakes with butter and honey simple syrup.

Tomato Pie

Localize it

Swap out any of the herbs or cheeses. The Manchego in this recipe is salty, and the mozzarella melts really well, so just keep that in mind when you're doing your swaps.

My mom makes her famous tomato pie every August when all the sweet, vine-ripened tomatoes are overflowing in her garden. This recipe pairs those juicy tomatoes with tangy cheese, fresh herbs, and a flaky crust. I can't think of a better way to enjoy the flavors of the season. Of course, a slice of pie should be accompanied by a glass of your favorite sparkling beverage and good company to share the occasion with.

FOR THE CRUST
2 cups all-purpose flour,
   plus a little extra for dusting
½ teaspoon salt
2 teaspoons dried parsley
13 tablespoons (1 stick plus
   5 tablespoons) cold unsalted
   butter, diced
6 tablespoons sour cream or
   plain full-fat yogurt
1 tablespoon white wine vinegar
¼ cup ice water

FOR THE FILLING AND ASSEMBLY
2 tablespoons cooking fat (page xv)
1 large onion, thinly sliced

2¼ pounds mixed heirloom tomatoes
   (mix of full size and cherries)
Salt
¾ cup hard salty cheese,
   such as Manchego or Parmesan
¾ cup shredded mozzarella cheese
¼ cup mayonnaise (page 33)
3 tablespoons chopped basil leaves
3 tablespoons chopped parsley
1 teaspoon chopped thyme
Salt and freshly ground black pepper
1 egg, beaten
1 tablespoon milk, cream, or water

Preheat the oven to 375°F.

Make the crust: In a large, wide bowl, combine the flour, salt, and parsley. Add the butter pieces and, using a pastry blender or your fingertips, cut them up and into the flour mixture until it resembles little pebbles. Keep breaking up the bits of butter until the texture is very coarse.

In a small dish, whisk together the sour cream, vinegar, and water, and combine it with the butter-flour mixture. Using a spatula or wooden spoon, stir the wet and the dry together until a shaggy dough forms. If needed, get your hands into the bowl to knead it a few times into one big ball. Pat the dough into a disk, wrap it in plastic, and chill it in the fridge for 1 hour or up to 2 days.

Make the filling: In a large skillet over medium, heat 1 tablespoon of the cooking fat. Add the onion and cook, stirring, until golden, about 15 minutes. Let cool.

Meanwhile, thinly slice the tomatoes; toss them with 1 teaspoon salt and let them drain in a colander for 30 minutes, tossing them occasionally.

In a bowl, combine the cheeses, mayo, 2 tablespoons each of the chopped basil and parsley, the thyme, a hefty pinch each of salt and pepper, and the sautéed onion.

Sprinkle a little flour in the bottom of a 10-inch well-seasoned cast-iron skillet. Set it aside.

On a lightly floured surface, roll the dough into a 13-inch circle. Fit it into the prepared skillet, allowing the edges to extend over the sides of the pan.

Spread the cheese mixture evenly over the bottom of the dough. Arrange the tomatoes on top. Gently fold the overhanging pie crust over the tomatoes. It doesn't have to be perfect.

Drizzle the pie with the remaining 1 tablespoon cooking fat and season with pepper. In a small bowl, whisk together the beaten egg and milk. Brush the crust with this egg wash, place the cast-iron pan on a rimmed baking sheet (to protect the bottom of your oven from any overflowing filling), and bake the pie until the tomatoes are browned, 50 to 60 minutes. Top the pie with the remaining 1 tablespoon each basil and parsley.

Summer Watermelon Picnic Salad

SERVES 4 TO 6
AS A SIDE

Localize it

If you can't find fresh watermelon, try swapping in a summer berry or even stone fruit. Both will pair well with summer tomatoes and fresh herbs. You can substitute the basil with fresh parsley, mint, or even dill. Can't find local feta? Ricotta, goat cheese, crème fraîche, or even plain whole milk yogurt will work well.

When the watermelons first start ripening at our farm, it feels like summer has officially arrived. The sweet, juicy watermelon cubes are so delicious paired with the vine-ripened summer cherry tomatoes and feta cheese. Balsamic vinegar and fresh basil finish it off for a salad that's a picnic must-have! This dish travels well, so don't hesitate to take it to your next backyard BBQ or summer outing.

4 cups cubed watermelon
2 cups halved cherry tomatoes,
4 ounces feta cheese, cubed
¼ cup extra-virgin olive oil
3 tablespoons balsamic vinegar
¼ teaspoon crushed red pepper flakes
   (page 42)

2 teaspoons honey
½ cup chopped basil plus
   additional for garnish
Flaky salt and freshly ground black
   pepper

In a salad bowl, toss together the watermelon, tomatoes, and feta cheese.

In a glass jar, whisk the olive oil, balsamic vinegar, crushed red pepper flakes, and honey. Add the basil and season with salt and pepper.

Drizzle the vinaigrette over the salad. Sprinkle it with salt and pepper and additional basil just before serving.

Simple Zucchini and Leek Soup

SERVES 4

Localize it

Any type of summer squash will work just fine. Can't find summer leeks? Swap in onions or shallots. Any fresh herb can stand in for the dill.

This is a wonderful, simple, and satisfying soup. It utilizes the oftentimes over-abundant zucchini that floods the market stalls all summer long. The zucchini and leeks are a great flavor combination on their own, but the addition of fresh dill really ties this soup together. Pair it with some crusty sourdough bread (page 44) for dunking and a side salad for a complete meal.

¼ cup unsalted butter
¼ teaspoon crushed red pepper flakes (page 42)
2 large leeks, washed, trimmed, and thinly sliced (white and light green parts only)
3 large cloves of garlic, thinly sliced
¼ cup dry white wine
4 medium zucchini (about 2 pounds), peels left on, cut into ¼-inch-thick rounds

Salt and freshly ground black pepper
¼ cup minced dill, plus additional for garnish
2 cups bone broth or stock or water, plus additional to thin if needed (pages 30–31)
Flaky sea salt
Zucchini blossoms (optional)

In a large Dutch oven or heavy-bottom saucepan over medium heat, combine the butter, red pepper flakes, and leeks and sauté, stirring occasionally, for 8 to 10 minutes.

Add the garlic and continue to cook, stirring often, for about 1 minute longer. Add the wine and cook until most of the liquid has evaporated.

Stir in the zucchini and a hefty pinch each of salt and pepper. Cover the pan, and steam over medium-low heat for 8 to 10 minutes or until the zucchini is just tender.

Transfer the mixture to a high-speed blender and add the dill and broth. Blend the soup on high speed until it is very smooth, adding more liquid to reach the desired consistency if needed. Return the soup to the pot and keep it over low heat for about 10 minutes so all the flavors meld. Taste-test and adjust the seasonings as needed.

Ladle the soup into bowls and garnish with dill, sea salt, and zucchini blossoms, if using.

Caesar Salad with Brown Butter Croutons

SERVES 4

Localize it

This is best with romaine lettuce, but if you can't find local romaine, you can massage the dressing into kale, endive leaves, bok choy, or even shredded cabbage. Parmesan is the traditional cheese, but any local sharp, hard cheese will work just fine.

Who doesn't love a fresh, crunchy Caesar salad on a hot summer day? There's not a lot going on here: crisp romaine lettuce; tangy, creamy, salty dressing; a bit of Parmesan cheese; and the best homemade brown butter croutons. It's perfection in salad form.

6 anchovy fillets packed in oil, drained
2 cloves of garlic, one peeled and left whole, the other minced
Salt
2 large egg yolks
2 tablespoons red wine vinegar or lemon juice
¾ teaspoon Dijon mustard
½ cup olive oil, plus additional to thin if necessary

3 tablespoons finely grated sharp salty cheese, plus additional for serving
Freshly ground black pepper
3 tablespoons unsalted butter
1 clove of garlic, minced
3 cups torn 1-inch pieces sourdough bread (page 44)
3 romaine hearts, leaves separated

Preheat the oven to 375°F.

Chop together the anchovy fillets, garlic, and pinch of salt. Use the side of a knife blade to mash the mixture into a paste, then scrape it into a medium bowl. Whisk in the egg yolks, vinegar, and mustard. Gradually pour in the olive oil, adding it drop by drop to start, and whisking until the dressing is thick and emulsified. Whisk in the cheese. Season with salt and pepper and taste for seasonings.

Heat the butter and remaining garlic in a small pan over medium heat and cook, stirring often with a wooden spoon, until the butter is golden brown, the garlic is fragrant, and the mixture is bubbling a bit, about 3 minutes.

On a baking sheet, toss the torn bread with the browned butter, salt, and pepper. Bake, tossing occasionally, until golden, 12 to 15 minutes.

In a large bowl, toss the romaine leaves with the dressing and top with the croutons. Grate or shave extra cheese on top and serve.

Farmhouse Onion Rings

SERVES 4 TO 6

Localize it

Sorry, folks, I wouldn't change much here, but any variety of onion (sweet, red, or yellow) will be delicious!

With onions grown right in our backyard, fresh eggs from the neighbors' chickens, and milk from one hundred yards away, this is a great way to feel pretty darn proud of the ingredients that go into one of our favorite backyard BBQ side dishes. I contemplated baking these, but Taylor quickly vetoed that idea. Baked onion rings? What's the point? I agree. This version is made with local, high-quality ingredients, but we do use vegetable oil for frying. There's just no getting around that part. These babies are worth it.

1 cup buttermilk
1 cup all-purpose flour
Salt and freshly ground
    black pepper
Pinch of crushed red
    pepper flakes (page 42)

1 large sweet onion, sliced into
    ¼-inch-thick rings
Vegetable oil for frying
Herb Goat Cheese Dressing
    (page 36) for serving

Preheat the oven to 250°F.

Place the buttermilk in a medium bowl. Place the flour in another medium bowl and season it with salt, black pepper, and red pepper flakes. Working in batches, toss the onion rings in the flour mixture; shake off the excess. Dip them in the buttermilk, letting the excess drip back into the bowl. Return them to the flour and toss to coat again; shake off the excess.

In a large skillet over medium, heat 2 inches of oil. Add half the onions, making sure they're completely submerged, and cook until the underside is golden brown and lightly crisp, about 4 minutes. Flip the onions and continue to cook, flipping them occasionally, until both sides are a deep golden brown. This will take anywhere from 6 to 8 minutes. Using tongs, transfer the onion rings to paper towels; season them with salt and pepper. When they've drained, transfer them to a baking sheet and keep them warm in the oven until you've fried all the remaining onions.

Serve with herb goat cheese dressing.

Classic
Coleslaw

SERVES 4

Localize it

Try shredding iceberg lettuce instead of cabbage if you can't find any. Shredded beets would stand in well for carrots.

In my personal opinion, summer is not summer without this barbecue staple. Nothing beats a simple coleslaw, and the more basic, the better. While I contemplated adding interesting ingredients to this recipe to make it stand out a bit more, I resisted the urge because sometimes there's just nothing better than crunchy cabbage tossed with a slightly sweet, slightly tart, creamy dressing.

1 cup mayonnaise (page 33)
2 tablespoons apple cider vinegar
1 tablespoon honey
2 teaspoons Dijon mustard
Salt
Freshly ground black pepper

½ medium green cabbage,
   very thinly sliced (about 4 cups)
½ medium red cabbage,
   very thinly sliced (about 4 cups)
2 medium carrots,
   julienned or grated

In a large bowl, whisk together the mayonnaise, vinegar, honey, mustard, salt, and pepper. Add the green and red cabbage and carrots to the dressing and toss to coat. Cover the bowl and chill the slaw until you're ready to serve it.

Summer Corn and Fish Chowder

SERVES 4

Localize it

Swap onions for the leeks. If you don't eat pork, you can swap the bacon for a few tablespoons of butter (you'll want to add a bit more salt if you do this). Any hot pepper can stand in for the jalapeño. No cod? No problem— this would taste great with haddock, pollock, striped bass, trout, or even salmon.

It's hard to believe something so simple can still knock your socks off—but this chowder most certainly does. While a lot of chowder-style soups can feel too heavy (especially in the summer), this version remains light and fresh with in-season vegetables, a flaky fish, and plenty of fresh herbs.

4 slices thick-cut bacon, chopped

2 large leeks, washed, trimmed, and thinly sliced (white and pale green parts only)

1 jalapeño pepper, seeded and finely chopped

1 clove of garlic, chopped

½ teaspoon dried thyme

¼ teaspoon crushed red pepper flakes (page 42)

½ cup dry white wine

2 medium potatoes, cut into ½-inch chunks

3 cups chicken stock, plus more to thin if needed (page 31)

Salt and freshly ground black pepper

¾ pound cod, skin removed, chopped

2½ cups fresh corn kernels

1½ cups heavy cream

Fresh parsley or cilantro leaves for serving

In a large saucepan over medium heat, cook the bacon until it is crisp, about 4 minutes. Transfer it to a paper-towel-lined plate to drain. Pour out all but 2 tablespoons of the bacon fat and reserve it for another use.

In the same pan, sauté the leeks in the reserved 2 tablespoons bacon fat for 2 minutes. Add the jalapeño, garlic, thyme, and red pepper flakes; sauté for 1 minute. Add the wine and cook, stirring frequently, scraping up any browned bits from the bottom, until most of the liquid has evaporated.

Stir in the potatoes, stock, and salt and pepper; bring the mixture to a boil. Reduce the heat to medium-low and simmer for 10 minutes.

Stir in the fish, corn, and two-thirds of the bacon and simmer until the fish is lightly poached and cooked through, about 5 minutes. Stir in the cream and simmer for 5 minutes.

Ladle the soup into bowls and garnish it with the remaining fresh herbs and the remaining bacon.

Zucchini, Swiss Chard, and Chickpea Stew

SERVES 4

Localize it

You can swap leeks, scallions, or shallots for the onion, and really any hearty green—kale, collard greens, bok choy, spinach, beet greens, turnip greens, or radish greens—for the Swiss chard. Any white bean will work for the chickpeas. Homemade chicken stock or even water will work for the veggie stock (if you use water, season the soup with extra salt and pepper).

Whenever folks are looking for spinach in the heart of summer, I suggest that they give Swiss chard a try. It's similar in flavor and texture, plus you get the added bonus of the chard stems, which lend an extra layer of flavor and texture to any recipe. This soup utilizes the whole vegetable (leaves and stem) and is just the thing when you're craving a simple and nourishing meal.

1 bunch of Swiss chard with stems
2 tablespoons unsalted butter
  or olive oil
1 medium yellow onion,
  finely chopped
3 cloves of garlic, minced
2½ tablespoons fresh thyme leaves
1 bay leaf
½ cup dry white wine
1 medium green zucchini,
  sliced into half-moons about
  ½ inch thick

1 medium yellow zucchini,
  sliced into half-moons about
  ½ inch thick
4 cups vegetable stock (page 31)
Salt and freshly ground
  black pepper
2 cups cooked chickpeas
1 tablespoon fresh lemon juice
2 teaspoons grated lemon zest
Pinch of crushed red
  pepper flakes (page 42)

Separate the stems from the chard leaves. Finely chop the stems and set them aside. Slice the leaves thinly and set them aside. In a large pot over medium heat, melt the butter. Add the onion and cook, stirring occasionally, for about 5 minutes. Add the Swiss chard stems, garlic, thyme, and bay leaf. Cook for about 1 minute longer. Pour in the wine and bring the mixture to a boil. Reduce the heat to medium-high and cook until most of the liquid evaporates. Add the zucchini, stock, and a hefty pinch of salt and pepper. Bring the liquid to a boil again. Reduce the heat to medium-low and cook until the zucchini is tender, about 8 minutes.

Add the chickpeas and chard leaves. Continue to cook until the chard wilts down a bit. Season with the lemon juice, lemon zest, red pepper flakes, and additional salt and pepper.

Ladle into bowls and serve.

Green Beans with Herb Butter

SERVES 4 TO 6

Localize it

Try this same method using sugar snap peas.

If you're anything like me, when you're invited to someone's house for dinner, you want to bring a dish that isn't complicated to make and is easy to transport—but still impresses your host. Enter these simple green beans with herb butter. They're lovely served warm, at room temperature, or even cold, and they accompany a variety of mains so they're the perfect dish, no matter the occasion.

1 tablespoon salt
1 pound green beans,
stem ends removed

Herb Butter (page 34)

Bring a large pot of water to a boil and add the salt. Add the beans and cook for 2 minutes. Drain and then place the beans in a serving dish.

Scoop a generous tablespoon or two of the herb butter on top of the warm beans and toss to coat. If you decide to serve the beans cold, be sure to lightly warm the butter before tossing it with the beans.

Sweet Corn Frittata with Cherry Tomato Compote

SERVES 4 TO 6

I created a frittata for every season in this book for a reason: There's no better way to use up everything in your fridge. Besides, you can enjoy a frittata for any meal of the day . . . for breakfast with coffee, for lunch with a side salad, or for dinner with a serving of roasted or steamed vegetables. I happen to love this frittata because it celebrates two of my favorite summertime treats: sweet corn and tomatoes. The corn adds the perfect texture while the jamlike tomato compote adds a wonderful sweetness. Try spreading a little bit of the compote onto a slice of sourdough toast (page 44) and top it with goat cheese for an extra-special treat.

FOR THE CHERRY TOMATO COMPOTE

2 tablespoons olive oil
2 cloves of garlic, minced
2 cups cherry tomatoes
  (any variety will work)
¼ cup dry white wine
8 to 10 fresh basil leaves,
  thinly sliced
Healthy pinch of fine sea salt
Freshly ground black pepper

FOR THE FRITTATA

2 tablespoons cooking fat (page xv)
1 bunch of scallions, white parts
  and green parts diced separately
2 cloves of garlic, minced
1 medium potato, scrubbed and
  cut into ¼-inch chunks
2 cups fresh or thawed frozen
  corn kernels
4 large eggs
½ teaspoon crushed red
  pepper flakes (page 42)
4 ounces feta cheese, crumbled

Make the compote: Heat the oil in a medium-sized skillet over medium heat. Add the garlic and cook, stirring often, for about 1 minute. Add the tomatoes and cook, stirring occasionally, for about 2 minutes longer. Pour in the wine and cook until the wine is reduced by about half. Add the basil, salt, and pepper and continue to cook, stirring occasionally, until the tomatoes burst and become fragrant, 5 to 8 minutes. Remove from the heat and set aside the tomatoes in a bowl.

Make the frittata: Position an oven rack about 3 inches from the top and preheat the broiler.

In a 10-inch cast-iron skillet over medium, heat 1 tablespoon of the cooking fat. Add the diced white part of the scallions and the minced garlic and cook, stirring often, until fragrant, about 3 minutes. Add the potato and continue to cook, stirring occasionally, until the potato softens, about 10 minutes. Add the corn and continue to cook for about 2 minutes longer.

In a large bowl, whisk together the eggs, red pepper flakes, and half the feta cheese. Pour the egg mixture over the veggie mixture in the skillet and top with the remainder of the cheese. Stir in the potato mixture and the scallion greens.

Wipe out the skillet and, over medium-high, heat the remaining 1 table-spoon of cooking fat. Cook the frittata, lifting up the cooked egg around the edges with a rubber spatula to let the uncooked eggs flow underneath, 2 to 3 minutes. Reduce the heat to medium and cook, giving the pan a shake now and again, until the eggs are mostly set but the center is still slightly jiggly, 3 to 5 minutes more.

Transfer the frittata to the oven and broil until the top is golden brown, 2 to 3 minutes (keep a close eye on the frittata, as it can easily burn). Serve topped with the tomato compote.

Summer Herb Potato Salad

I love this lighter take on potato salad because it's bursting with herbs (there's nothing like the flavor of fresh dill!) and has a slight tang from the red wine vinegar. It pairs well with any grilled meat or fish dish and is perfectly acceptable to eat as a complete meal by itself if you feel so inclined.

SERVES 4

Localize it

Any herbs will work here. You could also add a handful of arugula for a light, peppery bite. Swap diced kohlrabi or Swiss chard stems for the celery and full-fat yogurt for the mayo if you're not a mayo fan or are fresh out.

3 pounds potatoes
3 tablespoons red wine vinegar
Salt and freshly ground
 black pepper
¾ cup mayonnaise (page 33)
3 scallions, white and green parts,
 thinly sliced

1 celery stalk, diced
1 small red onion, thinly sliced
¼ cup chopped parsley
¼ cup chopped basil
¼ cup chopped dill
Pinch of crushed red pepper
 flakes (page 42)

Bring a large pot of salted water to a boil and add the potatoes. Reduce the heat to medium-low and simmer until they are tender, about 15 minutes. Drain the potatoes and let them stand until they are cool enough to handle, about 20 minutes.

Cut the potatoes into ½-inch pieces. Place the potatoes in a large bowl. Toss them with the vinegar and season with salt and pepper. Add all the remaining ingredients; toss. Sprinkle with additional salt and pepper and taste for seasonings. Adjust as needed.

Serve at room temperature or chilled.

Quick Pickled Chard Stems

MAKES 1 PINT

Localize it

You can use this method and the brine mixture to quick-pickle bok choy stems, broccoli stems, or even celery.

Folks often ask us what the heck to do with the chard stems since most recipes call for using the greens only. Well, here's your delicious answer—quick pickled chard stems! They're addictively tangy, super crunchy, and a great addition to any salad, sandwich, or charcuterie board. Bonus, they're absolutely beautiful and make great hostess gifts!

1½ cups chopped chard stems
   (from about 1 large bunch of chard)
2 teaspoons brown mustard seeds
1 cup apple cider vinegar

3½ tablespoons honey
½ teaspoon salt
½ teaspoon peppercorns

Place the chopped chard stems in a pint-size mason jar and set it aside.

Toast the brown mustard seeds in a saucepan for about 1 minute. Add the vinegar, ½ cup water, the honey, and salt. Bring the mixture to a boil. Reduce the heat to low and simmer, stirring occasionally, until the honey has dissolved, about 3 minutes. Remove the pan from the heat, add the peppercorns, and let the brine cool for about 10 minutes.

Pour the brine over the chopped chard and cover the jar with a secure lid. Refrigerate for at least 4 hours before enjoying.

Store the pickled chard stems in an airtight container in the fridge for up to three weeks.

Grilled Peaches with Ricotta, Honey, and Thyme

This dish is by far one of my favorite ways to enjoy the simple pleasure of ripe summer peaches. Grilling the peaches brings out even more of their natural sweetness, and this creamy, earthy thyme, honey, and ricotta topping simply cannot be beat.

1 cup whole milk ricotta cheese
2 tablespoons honey, warmed until pourable, plus more for serving
Leaves from 2 sprigs thyme, plus more for garnish

4 peaches, sliced in half, pits removed
2 tablespoons melted unsalted butter or oil
Salt
Ground cinnamon

Localize it

Any stone fruit will work here—plums, apricots, nectarines. You could swap in any woody herb for the thyme, such as sage, rosemary, or marjoram. Goat cheese or a thick full-fat plain yogurt could stand in for the ricotta.

In a medium-sized bowl, combine the ricotta, honey, and thyme. Mix well.

Heat an outdoor grill to high.

Meanwhile, brush the peaches with the melted butter or oil. Add them to the grill, cut side down. Grill the peaches, flipping them once during the cooking time, for 4 to 6 minutes or until they are golden brown and just cooked through.

Sprinkle each peach half with a pinch of salt and a dash of cinnamon. Top each with a spoonful of the ricotta mixture, then drizzle it with additional honey. Serve warm.

Grilled Zucchini with Herb Yogurt

Localize it

Any type of summer squash will work well here. Swap in goat's milk yogurt for a slightly tangier sauce. Use any fresh herbs you have on hand for the sauce.

Cooking zucchini on the grill yields the perfect texture—the outside gets lightly charred crisp while the inside stays tender. I like to serve this dish alongside a simple protein like grilled steak, chicken, or fish; leftovers can be added to a grain bowl for lunch the next day.

1 cup plain full-fat yogurt
2 tablespoons minced dill
¼ cup minced red onion
Pinch of crushed red pepper flakes
2 tablespoons red wine vinegar

Salt
2 pounds medium zucchini, sliced lengthwise into ½-inch-thick planks
2 tablespoons extra-virgin olive oil
Freshly ground black pepper

Preheat an outdoor grill to medium-high.

In a medium-sized bowl, combine the yogurt, dill, onion, red pepper flakes, vinegar, and a pinch of salt. Stir until the sauce is smooth. Taste for seasonings and adjust as needed. Cover, and refrigerate it until you're ready to use it.

In a large bowl, toss the zucchini with the oil and a pinch each of salt and pepper.

Grill the zucchini planks for 1 to 2 minutes on each side, until the outside is charred but the flesh is still firm. Using tongs, transfer the zucchini to a platter and drizzle it with the herb yogurt mixture.

Serve the zucchini immediately with extra sauce on the side.

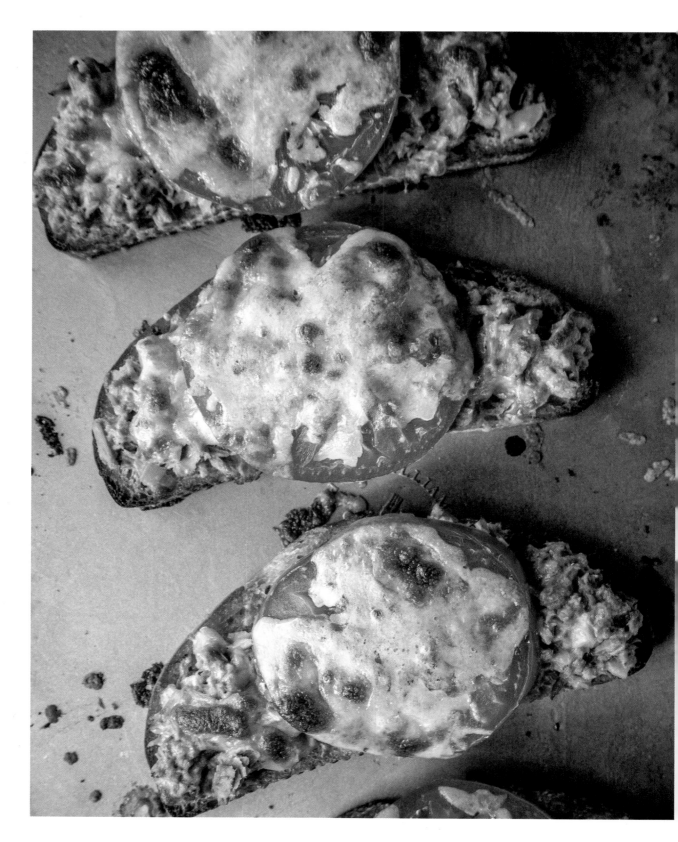

Sheet Pan Tuna, Tomato, and Sauerkraut Melts

SERVES 4

Localize it

Any canned or precooked white fish will work. You can even try these with cooked and shredded chicken breast for a totally different style but equally tasty melt. Try diced kohlrabi in place of celery for a similar crunch (I've done this many times when our celery crop is subpar or nonexistent, and it's delightful!). Full-fat yogurt in place of mayo is lovely. Parsley instead of dill is another great option.

When I was growing up, my dad would make tuna melts all the time. If I remember correctly, he would even crumble some potato chips over the top. So good! In this version, I've left my melts open-faced, and instead of chips, I've used a ripe but firm slice of garden tomato and a few spoonfuls of sauerkraut for added crunch and flavor. And while I must admit I'll always have a place in my heart for Dad's version, I can really get on board with this locally inspired take.

2 (5-ounce) cans tuna, drained
¼ cup mayonnaise (page 33), plus additional for spreading on bread
1 celery stalk, chopped (about ¼ cup)
½ a small red onion, chopped (about ¼ cup)
2 tablespoons red wine vinegar
1 tablespoon extra-virgin olive oil
1 tablespoon Dijon mustard
Salt and freshly ground black pepper

Pinch of crushed red pepper flakes (page 42)
1 tablespoon chopped parsley
1 tablespoon chopped dill, plus additional for garnish
4 slices sourdough bread (page 44), lightly toasted
½ cup sauerkraut, drained
4 tomato slices (from 1 large tomato)
4 slices aged cheddar cheese or another hard, slightly salty cheese

Preheat the broiler to high.

In a large bowl, combine the tuna, mayo, celery, red onion, vinegar, olive oil, mustard, salt, and pepper, red pepper flakes, parsley, and dill. Stir to combine, breaking up the tuna as you mix.

Place the bread on a baking sheet. Spread a thin layer of mayo over each slice. Divide the tuna mixture among the slices, then top it with 2 tablespoons of the sauerkraut followed by a slice of tomato and a slice of cheddar.

Broil until the cheese is melted and browned in spots, 3 to 4 minutes. Top with additional dill and more black pepper.

White Bean Chicken Chili

Localize it

Use any type of hot or sweet pepper; swap in goat's milk yogurt for cow's milk.

The beauty of using a whole chicken for this chili is that the broth makes itself and you can save any additional meat from the excess. This is such a nice meal to prepare when you're working all day, because everything gets tossed in the slow cooker, and all the magic happens while you're away doing more important things than standing in your kitchen stirring a pot of stew (though that just so happens to be one of my favorite activities). Leftovers are even better the next day, and this recipe makes quite a bit, so if you're not cooking for a crowd, you'll be able to enjoy this chili all week long or stash a few servings in the freezer.

1 pound dried navy beans, soaked in water for 8 hours or overnight
1 whole chicken (about 3 pounds)
Salt and freshly ground black pepper
2 large yellow onions, diced
6 large cloves of garlic, diced
1 tablespoon ground cumin
1½ teaspoons dried oregano
2 large poblano peppers, seeded and finely chopped

2 jalapeño peppers, diced (remove the seeds if you're sensitive to heat—we like it, so we keep some of the seeds)
Pinch of cayenne pepper (optional)
2 bay leaves
5½ cups bone broth or chicken stock (pages 30–31)
Plain full-fat yogurt for serving
Minced parsley for serving

Drain the soaked beans and set them aside. Pat the chicken dry with paper towels and sprinkle it generously with salt and pepper.

To the bowl of a large (8-quart) slow cooker, add the onions, garlic, cumin, oregano, peppers, cayenne, bay leaves, drained beans, and plenty of salt and black pepper. Give the mixture a little stir. Pour in the broth and 2 cups water. Top the whole darn thing with the chicken and cover. Cook the chili on low for 8 hours.

When you're ready to eat, remove the whole chicken from the pot, fish out the bay leaves, and use forks to shred the meat. Add half to the pot and give the chili a stir. Taste for seasonings and adjust as needed. Add more chicken if you feel like it needs it, and reserve the rest for salad, tacos, or any other use later in the week.

Ladle the chili into bowls and top it with a dollop of yogurt and plenty of minced parsley.

Zucchini and Corn Frittata

Localize it

Any summer squash works well here, as will any type of cheese. Swap the corn for cherry tomatoes or throw in a couple of hot peppers for some spice. Just keep the ratio of veggies, eggs, and cheese the same.

This simple summer frittata is a great way to use up the abundance of zucchini and fresh sweet corn that starts to pile up by midsummer. Try serving it with a salad of simply dressed greens topped with a little goat cheese for a complete meal.

2 tablespoons cooking fat
   (page xv)
½ small red onion, thinly sliced
2 cloves of garlic, thinly sliced
Pinch of crushed red
   pepper flakes (page 42)

1 zucchini, thinly sliced
1 cup fresh corn kernels
Salt
8 large eggs
¼ cup ricotta cheese

Set an oven rack 5 inches from the heat and preheat the broiler.

In a 10-inch cast-iron skillet over medium, heat the cooking fat and cook the onion, garlic, and red pepper flakes, stirring, until they are tender and fragrant, about 5 minutes. Add the zucchini and corn and cook until the vegetables are tender, about 7 minutes more. Season with salt.

In a bowl, whisk the eggs with a pinch of salt and pour them into the skillet with the vegetables. Cook the frittata over medium-high heat, lifting the cooked egg around the edges with a rubber spatula to let the uncooked eggs flow underneath, 2 to 3 minutes.

Reduce the heat to medium and cook, shaking the pan occasionally, until the eggs are mostly set but the center is still slightly jiggly, 3 to 5 minutes more.

Dollop the top of the frittata with the ricotta, transfer the skillet to the oven, and broil until the edges are golden brown and the eggs are set, 2 to 3 minutes. (Keep a close eye on the frittata, as it can easily burn if left in too long.)

Plate and serve warm.

Grilled Bread and Marinated Tomato Salad

SERVES 6
AS A SIDE

Localize it

I wouldn't change much here, as the ingredients should be easy enough to find in high summer in most places. However, you can swap out the balsamic vinegar for red wine vinegar, basil for parsley or dill, and scallions for the red onion.

This is a riff on panzanella, the popular Italian bread salad. It's a lovely dish to showcase summer tomatoes in all their sweet, juicy glory. With day-old bread (slightly stale bread absorbs the juices really well and keeps a nice texture), bold balsamic vinegar, and fresh herbs, this is a salad to celebrate the flavors of summer.

2 cloves of garlic, minced

5 ripe tomatoes, cored, seeded, and cut into quarters

1 pint cherry tomatoes, sliced in half

1 small red onion, minced

⅓ cup extra-virgin olive oil, plus additional for brushing

2 tablespoons balsamic vinegar

Salt and freshly ground black pepper

8 ounces day-old sourdough bread (page 44), cut into ¾-inch-thick slices

¼ cup chopped fresh basil

Oil your grill racks and preheat the grill to high.

In a large bowl, toss the garlic, tomatoes, onion, olive oil, and vinegar together. Season with a bit of salt and pepper and set aside for 20 minutes.

Brush the bread slices with olive oil. Place them on the grill, close the lid, and cook, turning them once, until they are well marked, about 4 minutes—but check the bread after 2 minutes, as this could happen faster, depending on your grill. Remove the bread to a cutting board, and when it is cool enough to handle, cut or tear it into ¾-inch cubes.

Add the bread to the bowl with the tomatoes and toss in the basil. Mix well until the bread cubes are evenly coated and serve. ·

Honey Jalapeño Corn Bread

SERVES 8

Localize it

I wouldn't change much here, but you can substitute cayenne peppers for the jalapeños (note that the cayenne will be a bit spicier) and pure maple syrup for the honey if you've got a good local source.

Every time I make corn bread, I think to myself, *I should make corn bread more often!* It's so easy to prepare and goes well with many summertime dishes, from chili to ribs to corn chowder. It's also pretty heavenly when warmed up in the oven and simply topped with a dollop of butter and a drizzle of hot honey. That's a dreamy farmer's breakfast for me!

Butter or oil for greasing
1 cup buttermilk
⅔ cup honey
2 large eggs, at room temperature
¼ cup unsalted butter, melted
1¼ cups all-purpose flour
1 cup yellow cornmeal
1 teaspoon salt

1 teaspoon baking powder
¼ teaspoon baking soda
2 jalapeño peppers, diced (Remove half to three quarters of the seeds if you are sensitive to heat.)
Drizzle of hot honey for serving (optional; page 194)

Preheat the oven to 375°F. Grease an 8-inch cast-iron pan with butter or oil.

In a medium bowl, whisk together the buttermilk, honey, eggs, and butter until the honey is fully incorporated.

In a large bowl, whisk together the dry ingredients.

Pour the wet ingredients into the dry and thoroughly mix the two together. Fold in the jalapeño peppers. Pour the batter into the prepared pan and bake for 25 to 30 minutes, until the corn bread is golden brown. Cool it in the pan for 5 minutes before slicing and serving. Drizzle each slice of corn bread with a little hot honey for added sweetness and spice.

Swiss Chard Pasta with Toasted Hazelnuts and Parmesan

SERVES 4 TO 6
AS A SIDE

Localize it

You can use kale instead of chard, and any nut will work in place of the hazelnuts. Fresh out of balsamic vinegar? Red wine vinegar or freshly squeezed lemon juice will work.

This is a light pasta dish, filled with ribbons of fresh chard and tossed with a little garlic-infused butter and balsamic vinegar. Toasted hazelnuts impart a subtle sweetness and a lovely crunch that's complemented perfectly by the sharp, salty bite of Parmesan shavings. It's a delicious combination, and also a really pretty pasta salad.

¼ cup hazelnuts
1 pound bow tie pasta (farfalle)
8 tablespoons unsalted butter, plus more if needed
4 cloves of garlic, minced
Hefty pinch each of salt and freshly ground black pepper

Small pinch of crushed red pepper flakes (page 42)
1 bunch Swiss chard, stems finely chopped and greens thinly sliced
4 ounces Parmesan cheese, shaved
2 tablespoons balsamic vinegar (optional)

Add the hazelnuts to a small skillet over medium heat. Toast them slowly, shaking the pan often, until lightly browned, 8 to 10 minutes. Remove them from the skillet, and when they are cool enough to handle, roughly chop the nuts.

Bring a large pot of salted water to a boil and cook the pasta until al dente. Drain it, reserving ½ cup of the cooking liquid and add it to a large bowl.

In a large skillet, heat the butter over medium-low heat. Once the butter begins to foam, add the garlic and use a wooden spoon to stir the mixture constantly until the butter begins to brown and have a slight nutty aroma, about 5 minutes. Add the salt, black pepper, and red pepper flakes. Give the mixture a good stir, and then set it aside to infuse for about 5 minutes longer away from the heat.

Pour the butter mixture (scraping the garlic, salt, pepper, and red pepper flakes) all over the warm pasta. If the pasta feels a bit dry, add a touch of the reserved cooking liquid. Toss to combine and set aside.

Set the same skillet (without cleaning it) over medium-high heat. Add the chard stems and cook for 5 minutes. Add the chard leaves and continue to cook, tossing the mixture every so often, until the greens begin to wilt and turn bright green, 3 to 5 minutes longer. Add a touch more butter or oil to the pan if it dries out too much.

Add the Swiss chard and hazelnuts to the pasta and toss it all together. Add the Parmesan shavings and the balsamic vinegar (if you're using it); toss. Taste for seasonings and add more salt and pepper if needed.

Serve warm or at room temperature.

Farm Stand BLTs with Spiced Garlic Mayo

SERVES 4

Localize it

You could use arugula or spinach instead of the lettuce, and any good mayonnaise or aioli will do.

No summer can pass by without a proper farm-fresh BLT. With good-quality bacon, vine-ripened tomatoes, crisp lettuce, and a tasty homemade garlic mayo, this BLT is a great example of what can happen when a few simple ingredients come together perfectly. These humble sandwiches are so delicious, they're good enough to serve for company!

12 slices thick-cut bacon
8 slices sourdough bread
  (page 44)
½ cup mayonnaise (page 33)
¼ teaspoon chili powder
¼ teaspoon ground cumin
1 small clove of garlic, minced
Salt

2 large farm-fresh tomatoes,
  sliced
2 heads butter lettuce or
  any type of fresh lettuce
Flaky sea salt
Freshly ground black pepper
Crushed red pepper flakes
  (page 42)

Preheat the oven to 350°F. Line a rimmed baking sheet with foil and set a wire rack inside.

Arrange the bacon on the rack, overlapping the slices if needed. Bake until they are crisp and the fat is mostly rendered, 20 to 25 minutes. No need to flip the bacon. Pour the bacon fat into a mason jar and refrigerate it for another day.

Turn the oven up to broil and place a rack in the uppermost position. Broil the bread slices for about 1 minute per side or until they are lightly browned.

In a small bowl, mix the mayo with the spices, garlic, and a pinch of salt. Taste for seasonings and adjust as needed.

To assemble the sandwiches, spread a generous layer of the garlic mayo onto each slice of bread, followed by a few slices of tomato, 3 slices of bacon, and lettuce. Sprinkle with flaky salt, black pepper, and red pepper flakes. Top with another slice of bread and devour.

Grilled Baby Back Ribs with Honey BBQ Sauce

SERVES 6

Localize it

Any ribs will work here.

We were so happy with the meat from our pig harvest last year, and while we quickly ate up a lot of chops, loins, roasts, and bacon (oh, the bacon went fast!!), we rationed the ribs for just the right occasion. And for us, that was Taylor's birthday. We invited some of our nearest and dearest friends and family over for a BBQ and served these ribs up alongside a table full of baked beans, coleslaw, and corn bread (pages 70, 245, and 271). I love firing up the barbecue for these delicious baby back ribs. They're simple to prepare, and the honey BBQ sauce is divine.

FOR THE RIBS
3 pounds country-style pork ribs
½ teaspoon salt
½ teaspoon freshly ground
   black pepper

FOR THE BBQ SAUCE
⅔ cup honey ketchup (page 37)
½ cup apple cider vinegar

¼ cup honey
2 teaspoons paprika
1 teaspoon ground cumin
1 teaspoon salt
1 teaspoon freshly cracked
   black pepper

Prepare the ribs: Put the ribs in a large pot or Dutch oven and sprinkle them with salt and pepper. Add enough water to cover; bring it to a boil. Reduce the heat, cover the pot, and simmer the ribs for 1 hour or until the ribs are tender (you can test them by inserting a fork or knife into one of the ribs); drain them.

Meanwhile, make the BBQ sauce: Combine the remaining ingredients in a medium-sized bowl and whisk well, until they are fully incorporated. Taste for seasonings and adjust as needed.

Preheat an outdoor grill to medium. Grill the ribs, uncovered, for 10 to 12 minutes, basting them with sauce and turning them occasionally.

Serve the ribs warm with additional sauce.

Fresh Corn and Tomato Salad

SERVES 6
AS A SIDE

Localize it

White wine, balsamic, or even apple cider vinegar will work well in place of the red wine vinegar. Any type of hot pepper can stand in for the jalapeño (or use crushed red pepper flakes, page 42). Swap the red onion for scallions or shallots. Any type of soft cheese or herbs you can get your hands on will be wonderful.

One of our favorite ways to eat in-season sweet corn is straight off the cob in the field (no cooking necessary!). Our second-favorite way is in this simple salad. Between the fresh corn and juicy, ripe tomatoes, this bright salad feels like summertime in a bowl. It's easy to whip up, travels well, and is the perfect accompaniment to just about any summer meal. If there are any leftovers, good news: It tastes even better the next day!

3 tablespoons red wine vinegar
Hefty pinch each of salt and freshly ground black pepper
¼ cup extra-virgin olive oil
6 ears fresh sweet corn
2 cups halved cherry tomatoes

8 ounces goat cheese, crumbled
1 small jalapeño pepper, seeded and thinly sliced
½ a medium-sized red onion, finely chopped
1 cup thinly sliced, fresh basil leaves

In a small bowl, whisk together the vinegar, salt, and pepper. Gradually whisk in the oil until the dressing is smooth.

Shear off the corn kernels with a sharp knife over a large bowl (you should have about 4 cups). Add the tomatoes, goat cheese, jalapeño, and onion to the bowl. Pour the vinaigrette over the salad and toss to coat. Cover the bowl and let the salad marinate for at least 30 minutes and up to 2 hours (the longer it marinates, the more flavorful it will be).

Right before serving, top with fresh basil.

Steak and Potato Kebabs with Chimichurri Butter

SERVES 6 TO 8

Localize it

Use any kind of meat here—lamb, venison, bison, or even a lean white meat like chicken or rabbit. Use any herbs you have on hand as well.

Growing up, every Friday night we had steak and baked potatoes for dinner. We always loaded up our baked potatoes with butter, chives, and plenty of salt and pepper. These kebabs take me back to those childhood flavors, with a little bit more grown-up sophistication in the form of an herby marinade for the steak and a dollop of fresh chimichurri butter to melt over the whole thing.

1 or 2 tablespoons chimichurri sauce (page 33)
½ cup (1 stick) unsalted butter, softened to room temperature
1 pound baby potatoes
¼ cup olive oil
2 tablespoons red wine vinegar
1 tablespoon chopped rosemary leaves

1 tablespoon chopped thyme leaves
2 cloves of garlic, minced
Salt and freshly ground black pepper
2 New York strip steaks, about 1¼ inches thick (2 pounds), cut into 1-inch chunks
6 to 8 wooden skewers

Begin soaking the wooden skewers in water about 15 minutes before you are ready to make the kebabs. Preheat the grill to medium-high.

In a small bowl, combine the chimichurri with the butter.

Bring a large pot of salted water to a boil and cook the potatoes until they are just tender and parboiled, 3 to 5 minutes; drain them well.

In a small bowl, whisk together the olive oil, vinegar, rosemary, thyme, and garlic; season with salt and pepper to taste. Set aside.

Season the steak cubes with salt and pepper.

Thread the potatoes and steak cubes onto the skewers; brush them with the herb and oil mixture.

Grill the skewers, turning them occasionally, until the steak is cooked through to the desired doneness, 8 to 10 minutes.

Serve the kebabs warm with the chimichurri butter.